First published in 2020 by Bluetrain Publishing
Ltd in arrangement with Trek Bicycle Corporation.

bluetrainpublishing.com

Editors: Guy Andrews and Taz Darling
Art direction: Bluetrain
Book design: Alex Fergusson and Ultan Coyle
Copy editor: Claire Read
Jefa de Producción: Virginia Hernando
Reprographics and color: Keith George

Printed and bound in Spain by SYL

ISBN 978-1-8380763-0-6

For my mother, Saloma Elizabeth Fisher (1929-2020)
Who always believed in me, supported me and patiently explained everything to me.

Gary Fisher

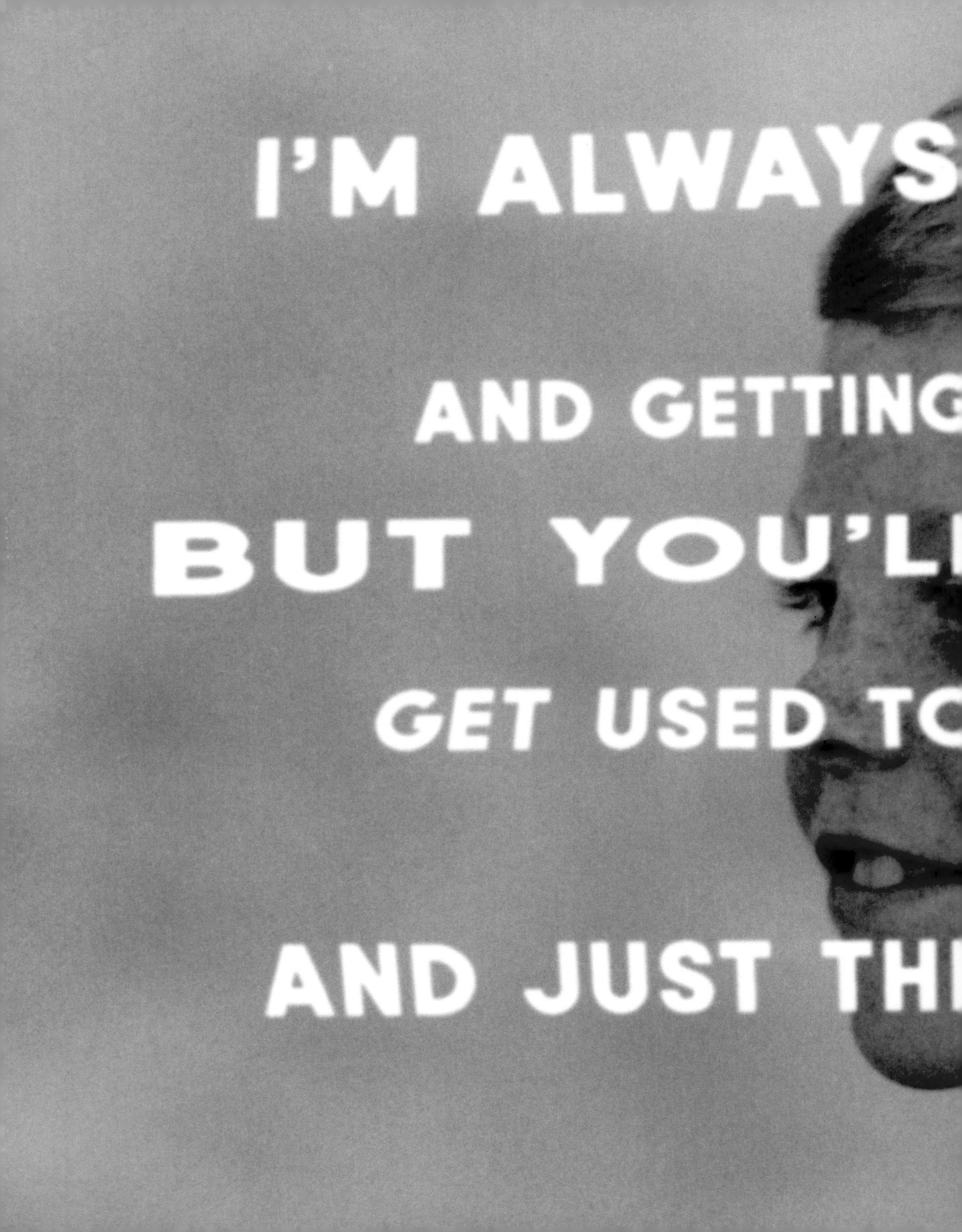

I'M ALWAYS

AND GETTING

BUT YOU'LL

GET USED TO

AND JUST TH

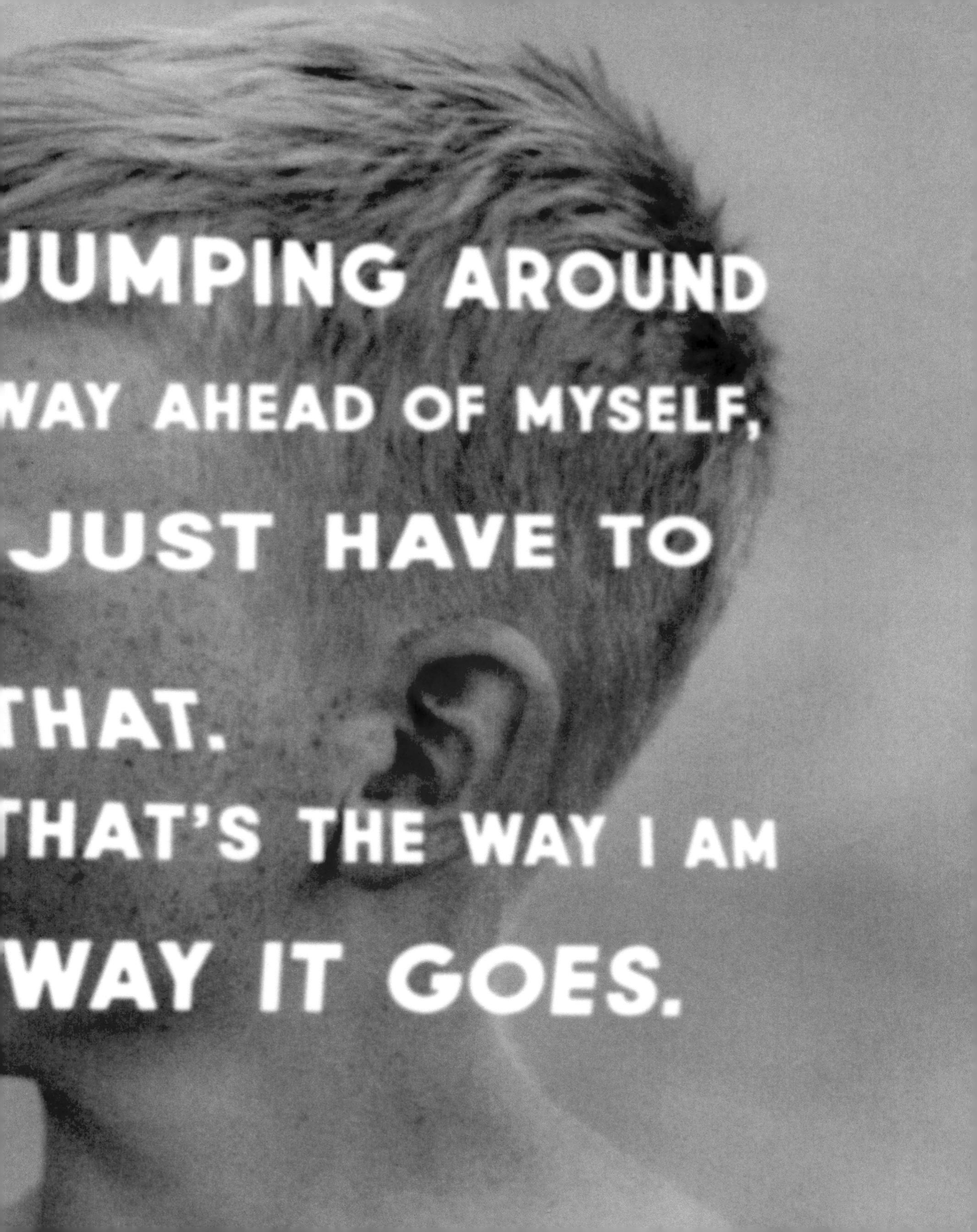

JUMPING AROUND
WAY AHEAD OF MYSELF,
JUST HAVE TO
THAT.
THAT'S THE WAY I AM
WAY IT GOES.

It's inevitable that stories about you always start long before you were even born. With the world you are born into and the people who mold and make you. I guess I got pretty lucky with the people who laid the tracks for me to follow.

My great-grandfather, Vincent James 'VJ' Applegate, literally laid down tracks because, among a bunch of other stuff – including mining and working the oil fields in Montana – he built rail-roads. We grew up listening to stories about what he did and how. There was some crazy stuff and some sad stuff but what I really remember and learned from the stories was how he treated people right. That sounds pretty normal now but you've got to remember that, back in his day, normality for the 'Coolies' and 'Navvies' working in camps was terrible, racist gang master-controlled conditions. He stood out because he had a reputation for treating his Chinese and Irish laborers very well. Not just by western standards, but also by learning what was important to them and respecting it, and in return they worked really hard for him.

YOU'VE GONE TO MEET THESE GUYS BECAUSE YOU RESPECT THEIR SKILLS AND THEIR ABILITIES AND YET YOU'RE NOT PREPARED TO RESPECT THEIR CULTURE?

THAT'S JUST STRAIGHT UP RUDE AND ARRO-GANT.

Growing up around these stories taught me that you always need to respect cultures and the way different people do things. It's often the smallest things that mean a big deal. I mean, now you tell anyone who's got a meeting with someone from China, Taiwan or Japan about the whole business card exchange and bowing ceremony thing. It's stuff like being able to sit on your haunches when you talk with them. It seems odd to us but that's how some folks naturally sit for a meeting. If you make that effort to be respectful and literally engage at that level, then it makes a big difference. You've gone to meet these guys because you respect their skills and their abilities and yet you're not prepared to respect their culture? That's just straight up rude and arrogant. But I know a lot of people who'd think that you couldn't possibly have a meeting like that, that it was primitive or some such bullshit and that's why some companies have a bad experience out there. It's actually a really cool way to sit, I can do it for hours on end still. I was lucky to be schooled early in that kind of thing by my Japanese aunt and my Japanese friends.

LIKE, IF YOU'VE GOT THE CHANCE, WHY WOULD YOU NOT GO AND MEET THE PEOPLE WHO ACTUALLY MAKE YOUR SHIT ?

I also know people who'd never go into the back rooms or workshops, because it's beneath them somehow. Like, if you've got the chance, why would you not go and meet the people who actually make your shit? It's not just basic humanity, it's good business sense. I learned pretty early that your bike is only as good as the last wrench that touches it, and these are the wrenches and welding torches that can make or break you. If they think you're a shit head, or have no idea who you are, then they won't care and you'll get shit product and you'll deserve it. If you make sure the people who are actually hands-on with your stuff are happy then they'll be happy making it and they'll care about the quality. That connection with people is crucial and there's a whole lot of that – of both getting it right and getting it wrong – in this story.

Those stories about the railroad days also taught me that being too easy on people can be a mistake too. The Italian stonemasons who were crucial to building the tunnels my great-grandfather needed essentially held him to ransom, and his whole railroad project never made any money because of them. The Italians I've worked with have been totally awesome, but again you've got to respect the fact that they can think very differently. Anyone trying to get product out of them just before they go on vacation for the whole of August will tell you that! But they're also amazingly friendly and creative as a nation. Paola Pezzo, who won Fisher Bikes the first ever mountain bike Olympic Gold medal, was incredible in her level of presentation and preparation. The late Dario Pegoretti, the famous framebuilder, was wonderful to spend time with too. He was the one who told me: "Never follow the market, make the market." I like to think this story will show I took that on board pretty well.

14

GREAT-GRANDPA LEAVITT, my mom's grandfather, was involved in the creation of the original San Diego transit system, which helped change it from a village into a thriving city. Back when I was hearing those stories, California was in its second age of post-war expansion, so I could really draw parallels. But most of all it showed me that one person can really be a big part of making a difference.

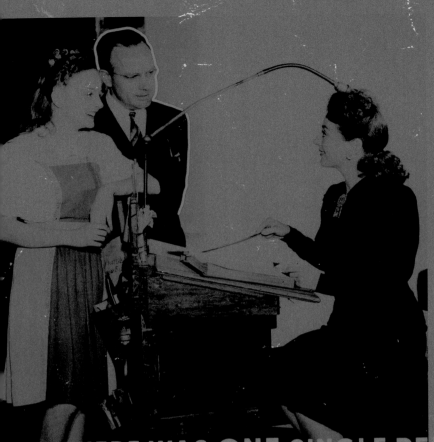

He was born in Iowa, grew up in Montana, but moved to LA when he was still in his teens to get away from the cold weather during the 1918 flu pandemic. He was the editor of his Hollywood high school newspaper. Right out of school he got a job with Hal B. Wallis, the seminal Hollywood publicist. He worked in publicity for 10 years, but the most significant job he had was to help actors transition from the silent movies to the talkies.

Fred had talked his way into a part-time job as a laborer at the Pickford-Fairbanks Studio while he was still at school. He was a quick learner and a great problem solver – maybe that's where I get it from – so he worked his way up through set building into more and more technical roles. That meant he was working in the sound departments in Hollywood when films went from silent to talkies and they needed scripts because, all of a sudden, actors needed to talk.

IF THERE WAS ONE SINGLE PERSON WHO MADE A MASSIVE DIFFERENCE TO THE WAY I THOUGHT AND HOW I APPROACHED THE WORLD THOUGH, I GUESS IT WAS MY GRANDFATHER ON MY MOTHER'S SIDE – FRED APPLEGATE. GROWING UP IN THE MIDDLE OF NOWHERE BUT SPEAKING IN THE SAME WAY AMERICANS FROM THE COASTS, HE REALISED WHAT A LOT OF THE CINEMA WORLD ACCEPTS AS 'ENGLISH'.

-(4) VINCENT JAMES APPLEGATE, James on the 1880 census, b. 25 oct. 1879 at Emerson, Mills County, Iowa, and was living with his family in Emerson, Iowa, [in?] of 1880 at the time of the census. He lived at ag[e] [...] (n t am [...] 11[...] d. s[...]ed [...] Feb 19[..] in [...] Francisco. He m. 25 June 1902 (9) SALOMA ALThEA GaRbERG, ceremony perform[...] by [...] n le, the Rev. [...] [...] n [...] e Meth dist Episcop[...] en s [...] e. Eli[...]t, [...] a T[...] emon [...] s w nes c [...] Loren Earle Garberg, Saloma's brother, and Marie [...] ppegate, Vincent [...] s at t. V. J [...] E[...] bec m[...] [...] [...]d Apple[...] t[...] ne[...] ona r [...] n rac [...]. They ar v[...] Los Angeles about 1946. He d. 26 Nov. 1958 from a ruptured aortic aneur[...]m [...] [...] te iosclr[...]s[...] r [...] ent [...] [...] re [...] e n Ceme[...]ry. [...] um [...] [...] GaRB[...] [...] L[...] A E d. [...] 52 T [...] d id was:

-(2) FRED WILLIAM APPLEGATE, (William Fred on his birth certificate) b. 5 April 1904 at Red Oak, Montgomery County, Iowa, m. 15 Sept. 1923 at Oakland CA (3) VIRGINIA LEAVITT, b. 28 Sept. 1904 at the Andrews Flat, West Wood St., Youngstown, Ohio, dtr. of (6) JOHN CALVIN LEAVITT and (7) ELIZABETH MOWREY (Lizzie on her daughter's birth certificate). Their children are:

-John Vincent Applegate, b. 10 June 1926 at Hollywood CA
-Fred William Applegate, b. 27 Jan. 1929 at Hollywood CA
-(1) SALOMA ELIZABETH APPLEGATE, b. 18 Nov. 1929 at Hollywood CA.

Sources:
      Family records of Saloma Applegate Fisher.
      [...] [...] C [...] [...] M [...] County, town of Emerson,

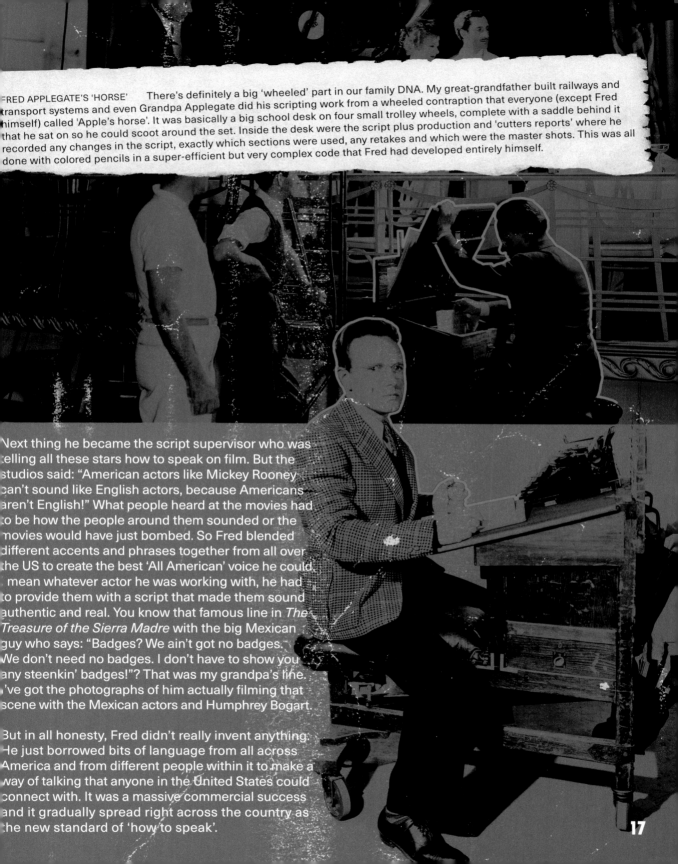

FRED APPLEGATE'S 'HORSE' There's definitely a big 'wheeled' part in our family DNA. My great-grandfather built railways and transport systems and even Grandpa Applegate did his scripting work from a wheeled contraption that everyone (except Fred himself) called 'Apple's horse'. It was basically a big school desk on four small trolley wheels, complete with a saddle behind it that he sat on so he could scoot around the set. Inside the desk were the script plus production and 'cutters reports' where he recorded any changes in the script, exactly which sections were used, any retakes and which were the master shots. This was all done with colored pencils in a super-efficient but very complex code that Fred had developed entirely himself.

Next thing he became the script supervisor who was telling all these stars how to speak on film. But the studios said: "American actors like Mickey Rooney can't sound like English actors, because Americans aren't English!" What people heard at the movies had to be how the people around them sounded or the movies would have just bombed. So Fred blended different accents and phrases together from all over the US to create the best 'All American' voice he could. I mean whatever actor he was working with, he had to provide them with a script that made them sound authentic and real. You know that famous line in *The Treasure of the Sierra Madre* with the big Mexican guy who says: "Badges? We ain't got no badges. We don't need no badges. I don't have to show you any steenkin' badges!"? That was my grandpa's line. I've got the photographs of him actually filming that scene with the Mexican actors and Humphrey Bogart.

But in all honesty, Fred didn't really invent anything. He just borrowed bits of language from all across America and from different people within it to make a way of talking that anyone in the United States could connect with. It was a massive commercial success and it gradually spread right across the country as the new standard of 'how to speak'.

17

"Grandpa Fred worked in Hollywood for almost 40 years from 1931. He worked on hundreds of movies and with stars like Humphrey Bogart, Joan Crawford and Basil Rathbone"

18

never realized it at the time but, looking back, Fred basically did with words what I did with bikes. I didn't invent the mountain bike — I just took all the best bits and tweaked them till they worked really well. I then packaged them up as something totally different to the uptight world of road biking and created something that people all over the world could understand and enjoy.

Another thing Fred was big into was physical condition and the knowledge that getting the most from your body and mind is really important. He was running, sea swimming and eating health foods when most people thought processed foods were the safer, healthier future. He was part of the Whole Earth Catalog movement right at the start and we used to go down to Los Angeles farmers markets and bring home all these wonderful, delicious things you'd never see anywhere else. What we sat down to eat was always interesting, because back then organic food included some pretty ugly stuff. But I've taken that whole health food thing with me throughout life. It was knowing about it that helped get a job catering for Grateful Dead, because they were all into health foods too.

My grandpa taught me that your body is an incredible thing and that letting it go to shit and be wasted is the biggest fallout of the whole 300 years of industrialization. Even now I'm 70, I still fight as hard as I can to stay in shape. If I can't make a bike go fast or fit into my suits then I'm pissed and I'm going to do something about it. And he showed me how sound is a really big part of the emotional environment we live in. That isn't just about music or technology; it's a base instinct. It's what we humans do. We control and enhance our environments, and noise and sound are really important for that. You can see it when you go way back into cultures all over the world. Sufis and witch doctors believed they could get into these trance-like dances just with the right noise and rhythm.

In my grandpa's case it was 'talkies' going to higher resolution. They changed the movie theaters at the same time, fitting much more powerful speaker systems so they didn't have to have be shaped to amplify a single human voice. He developed a lot of new technology around making sure these louder systems still sounded great. Inevitably those sound influences made it home and I still remember he had this bitchin' reel-to-reel tape with this killer hi-fi when I was five or six years old. My dad also had a really nice hi-fi with a Heathkit amplifier and that introduced me to the whole idea of modifying equipment, and even building totally new stuff, to get the results you needed. That meant I always wanted to have a really good hi-fi growing up, and I'd play around with it to get just the sound I wanted. Obviously that was all invaluable when I started working on the sound and light for the Grateful Dead shows, but being shown that you can make your own world and shape your own environment is always an incredibly powerful gift to give to anyone

I DIDN'T INVENT THE MOUN –TAIN BIKE

I JUST TOOK ALL THE BEST BITS AND TWEAKED THEM TILL THEY WORKED REALLY WELL. I THEN PACKAGED THEM UP AS SOMETHING TOTALLY DIFFERENT TO THE UPTIGHT WORLD OF ROAD BIKING AND CREATED SOMETHING THAT PEOPLE ALL OVER THE WORLD COULD UNDERSTAND AND ENJOY

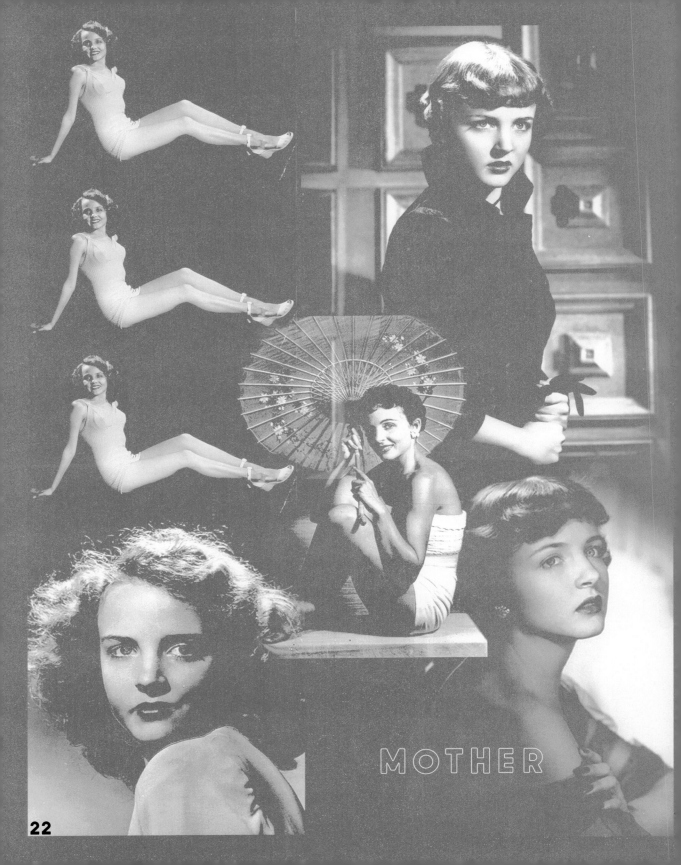

MOTHER

I was born in Oakland but my father was in the Navy so we moved to Guam when I was only six months old. My mom was called Saloma Fisher and she liked to sing. She was a wonderful singer, so she got work in the nightclubs over there and she caused a real scene. We didn't know until her 80th birthday that she'd pressed her own vinyl back in the day. She had promotional headshots done too and wore different outfits and make up for each shot – she looked incredible. It's obvious now that she was where I got my sense of the importance of that individual style. But my father went crazy about her working in the clubs so they split up and we ended up moving back to Beverly Hills and living with my grandparents, Fred and Virginia. That was a fantastic place to be. Because my grandpa worked in the movies there were actors and actresses coming round all the time, and my grandpa would take pictures with them and us. Not just snapshots but proper posed photographs that took maybe half an hour to compose because he always used to say: "There's no point in doing them unless they're going to be good!" I learned so much from him about making the most of every opportunity you get.

23

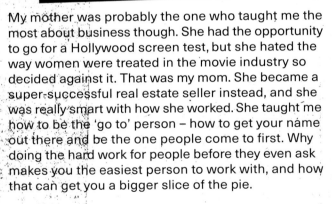

My mother was probably the one who taught me the most about business though. She had the opportunity to go for a Hollywood screen test, but she hated the way women were treated in the movie industry so decided against it. That was my mom. She became a super-successful real estate seller instead, and she was really smart with how she worked. She taught me how to be the 'go to' person – how to get your name out there and be the one people come to first. Why doing the hard work for people before they even ask makes you the easiest person to work with, and how that can get you a bigger slice of the pie.

My lessons started young. When I was a little kid, we used to go to a local park. The Disney family were often there too and Walt would be telling everyone about his plans to build this magical place for kids and families to visit. Anyway, we wind up being invited to the opening day and I take my best friend Arthur Robbins and it's amazing. So the very next day I'm over at Arthur's house and we build own version of Disneyland in his backyard. What does my mom do? She takes some pictures, contacts her friend at the *LA Times* and says: "Hey I've got a story for you..." She got my picture in the *LA Times* before I was even five years old because she saw it could be a fun story and she did the work for them. That's a big, big lesson right there.

'GIVE 'EM WHAT THEY WANT'

, 9, Runs Back yard Amusement Park

BEVERLY HILL
31—"I just give th
what it wants," sa
Robbins, "no mor
less. You keep yo
right and don't c
one, and

Se summe
us in ent realized $8.50 after
ed to order the park

cerned.
COMPLEX—
His amusement
tained exclusive
backyard of his

everly Hills Boy Runs
ear Yard 'Disneyland'

Four Young Playmates Co-operating in
Venture Netting $3.10 in Three Weeks

ttention Mr. Walt Dis-
You had best look to
r laurels.
t Beverly Hills way
ng Arthur Robbins, 9-
-old boy with the vitali-
and energy of a Mike
is on your trail with
own junior version of
eyland.
course his take won't
roximate the Anaheim
land for a couple of
s yet. In fact for the first
e weeks of operation,
ur reports a net profit
3.10. But he's a real

the Golden Gate bridge —
Robbins style—which even
Disneyland can't match.
Table tennis, dart games
and other "skill" games—
strictly legal, of course—dot
the area. In the center is a
portable swimming pool
which requires 8 cents ad-
mission and you furnish your
own towel.
With some of the profits
from the first day's rush business, Arthur procured a min-
iature golf set which now requires his father to keep his
automobile on the street at
nights. After all, only on

How It Started
Young Robbins, along
with four playmates, Kenny
Glass V; Mike Adelman, 8;
Hans Troesch, 9, and Gary
, 7, became bored just
tting around the house in
e running days of their
summer vacation. Arthur
osed they get into some

mother, Mrs. Rose Robbins,

ING TICKETS
play... ... 803 Willaman Drive,
Beverly Hills, into an amusement park.
First item to be completed
was a "scare ride." It con-
sists of a speedy trip around
the yard via wagon with Arthur and one of his partners
furnishing the manpower.

cou...
is i...
mo...
thur point...

Park's Top Treat
Top treat of the
amusement park
"grand tour" which takes
customers around the b
This is accomplished
when the "scare ride"
busy and Arthur can rele
the wag for a bi
lemona... ...n set... in a
his h es was
good... ...most of
the pro... ...replace
glasses ... ...y careless
customers.
Next year? Youngsters are
already planning a new at-
traction to separate playmates from their spending

25

Can't be bothered, Hop-a-longs on

Garry + Debby + the new chairs

Sometime in 1954 my mother went to visit my uncle Freddie at the University of California, Berkeley. It was there she met my stepdad, Robert Fisher, who was studying architecture. They fell in love straight away and ran away to Las Vegas to get married. When he graduated he took a job with Welton Becket Associates in San Francisco and we all moved to the Sunset district of the city. He taught me how to draw and how to see things technically but he was also a painter, an abstract impressionist, and San Francisco and New York were the scene for that. We've got four of his paintings at home, hanging in my wife's office. Along with being a successful architect he was a great photographer who won a lot of awards over the years. His company – Fisher Friedman – had the whole floor above this amazing Croatian fish restaurant called Tadich Grill, which is the oldest continuously operating restaurant in California. The offices were full of his photos. I mean they could be used for a separate book that would stand up as a classic all on its own. He used to say that taking great photographs is all about knowing when to pull the trigger. I've learned since that a whole lot of things are all about knowing just the right moment to pull the trigger.

26

Robert Fisher played a big part in creating the physical landscape that shaped the world we all grew up in, but not always in a good way. He was the architect for 30% of Orange County; he pretty much made the Californian suburbs. I mean he did also produce some pretty iconic buildings. Some of them are even still on T-shirts they're that well known; he was a leader in the social architecture experiment. He was a big part of changing the way people lived, how that related to their work, and how they moved around. He thought he was building a better world by getting people out of crowded, polluted inner cities, but in the process he created an environment where cars were king. A world where bikes were pretty much extinct unless you were a kid or a drunk who couldn't drive.

He actually created a lot of the issues that we're working so hard to solve now. But maybe if cycling had been more mainstream back then I wouldn't have gotten into it as a way to escape, to be different, to find myself. It certainly shows that trying to solve a problem isn't ever as simple as it looks and sometimes what looks like the right solution ends up being an even bigger issue than the original one.

Family   9/25   Fisher '54

Above all my parents' biggest gift to me is that they were really tolerant and open-minded. They didn't follow rules about what you can and can't do, were never judgmental, and they taught me to be the same. "Don't take things for granted." "Don't make presumptions about other people and how they got there." They said that all the time. "Listen a little bit, will you?" was their favorite response when I was getting heated up about something. I don't always manage to stick to that advice, but whenever I do things always end up going a lot better.

My friends also used to think that my parents were really cool, which was a big deal to me. Bohemian and artistic, my mom and stepdad were soon well known in the bike community for putting on the best parties. That was mostly because they had the best sound system, but also they just really liked all the bike scene people. At the races, my dad would take photographs that got used for newsletters and race posters. Poster art was really important in every scene back then and there were some incredible designers producing artwork for these little bike races. That's how I first met Rick Valicenti and he ended up doing catalogues for Trek. Peter Hoffman, a renowned graphic designer and poster artist of the time, designed the Tour of Nevada City poster using my father's photographs. That was the biggest race in California and that all happened totally independent of me. Those parties, photographs and posters were how my parents got involved with bike racing, and they were also a big part of how I got involved with Grateful Dead and the whole counterculture scene.

Writing all this down now, there are so many things that are obviously so relevant to the way I am and the way my life developed. My family and how they lived gave me really determined DNA, some amazing stories to learn from, and a fantastically free environment to grow up in. So I guess that's where we go next.

"DON'T MAKE PRESUMPTIONS ABOUT OTHER PEOPLE AND HOW THEY GOT THERE."

"FISHER YOUR HAIR'S TOO LONG"

I WAS A REAL OUTCAST, AN OUTSIDER

Being different started early. I was brought up differently and I just didn't do what the other kids did. That gave me real advantages and strengths later in life, but being different as a kid can be pretty hard and I certainly suffered a lot at the time because of it.

My mom's connections with the movies and the media meant I'd already gotten into the *LA Times* with the Disneyland hustle. I don't know anyone else who was in a major newspaper that young for doing something like that, but that was the world I was growing up in. Different.

Even the kids I hung out with from an early age were different. When I was five my best friend, who lived just round the corner, was Japanese. My uncle Don had been in the military in Japan and married our Japanese aunt out there and she was awesome, so hanging out with my buddy was cool as far as I was concerned. He used to have the best food too, so we used to swap and share lunches all the time. But you've got to remember that this was only 10 years after the end of the war and 14 years after Pearl Harbour and so the Japanese were still not at all popular in the US. Us two being seen together was a big deal to some people and a handful of them made that very clear.

It wasn't a big deal to me or my family, though, but then again my family didn't have a conventional attitude. We'd always made our own way and we were proud of that. After all, there was great-Grandpa Leavitt's creation of the San Diego transit system, and great-Grandpa Applegate founded a railroad and they both did contracting work in Idaho in the mining boom. Traditionally my family had done well, but the big scene and big money were a couple of generations back now.

"My brother Rick riding the mini racer I built for him"

MASTER COPY

"Here's Barney Pugh, Rick, me and Mike Reiney standing in front of Ray Andrews' car with Paragon bike and pink wheels"

THAT'S A REALLY LIBERATING GIFT. BEING ALLOWED TO THINK YOU CAN MAKE WHATEVER YOU NEED, NOT BEING TOLD YOU CAN'T DO IT OR IT'S EASIER TO BUY SOMETHING. IT WASN'T SOMETHING THAT MY PARENTS CONSCIOUSLY DID OR I WAS EVEN REALLY AWARE OF AT THE TIME, IT'S JUST THE WAY IT WAS. THAT'S SUCH A POWERFUL MINDSET TO BE BROUGHT UP WITH.

Grandpa Fred made a huge contribution to the movie business but he was still classed as a technician. That meant he didn't make much money, and what he did make he invested. So when we moved to San Francisco after my mother and father split we had no spare money. Luckily my stepfather was a really hands-on guy. I guess most people would buy stuff on credit or make do, but not my dad. He made a lot of our furniture and, because he was an architect and an artist, he had a real flair for design too. We weren't just sitting on boxes and eating off cable drums. I was maybe only six or seven years old but I can still vividly remember him making this amazing dining table out of an old door. Stripping it down and then building it up, filling the framework and polishing until it looked incredible. He made this crazy-looking rough textured cork coffee table as well. It had a two-inch-thick cork top with white picture framing trim around the outside. You'd kill for something like that in an art house auction today, but he just had the idea and built it up.

That was just the way he was. His family, who came from Sacramento, didn't have much money and so they made stuff when they needed it. They passed that attitude on to him and he passed it on to me.

33

Unfortunately that attitude – added to the fact I was obviously different in how I thought – didn't go down well in school and I had a pretty bad time. I was an easy target. How I dressed, how I acted and that I just wasn't interested in what the other kids were into and didn't pretend to be. That pissed them off. I was the littlest guy in school too so there was little danger in pounding on me. I was also kind of a loner so you weren't taking on a whole crew if you picked on me. That meant I got beat up all the time.

Riding bikes was my only escape and by this time I had a proper bike– an Italian Legnano with Campagnolo equipment. Before that I'd just been on a flat bar Sturmey-Archer machine that was pretty slow, so this new bike really opened up how fast and far I could ride. That Legnano was definitely my gateway into the whole cycling scene and luckily I'd joined just as it started getting a little stronger.

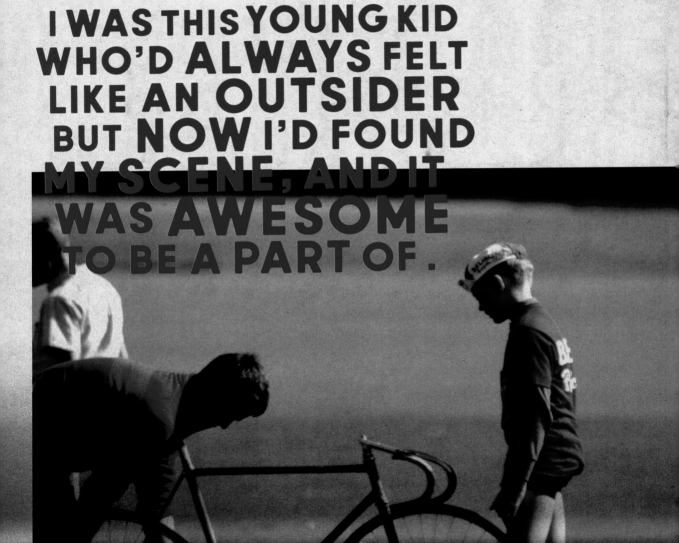

I WAS THIS YOUNG KID WHO'D ALWAYS FELT LIKE AN OUTSIDER BUT NOW I'D FOUND MY SCENE, AND IT WAS AWESOME TO BE A PART OF.

"1963. Racing with Antonio Gatto (left), one of the infamous Gatto Brothers, and Speedy Gonzales – I didn't know his name but that's what we called him. I'm riding a Masi bike bought from Dave Staub which he rode in the 1960 Rome Olympics."

California had once been a big deal on the US and even world cycling scene. The Rose Bowl in Pasadena hosted the Olympic track cycling in 1932 and the six-day races there were once huge events. You used to get Hollywood stars turning up to watch and be seen at the biggest events, but by the 1950s there was almost no racing going on. Come the '60s there was some track racing on TV in California and a makeshift track at The Polo Fields in Golden Gate Park, but it was still a tiny scene. I did some digging a while back and it turns out there were only around 120 bike racers in the whole of northern California with 66 seniors, 34 juniors, seven intermediates and just one woman. The scene may have been tiny, but it was also really enthusiastic and I got the bug. Then in '63 they built the Hellyer Park Velodrome in San Jose. It was only a 335-meter outside track but it instantly became the center of our racing universe.

Outside of the track there were a few local clubs. I rode for Belmont Bicycle Club and then Pedali Alpini but there were also the Berkeley Wheelmen, Club Endspurt and San Francisco Wheelmen. Seeing anyone else riding was so rare that you'd stop them and get their number and try and hook up for more rides. That's how I ended up as part of a group of young local riders: Barney Pugh, Mike Rainey and Steve Lubin. We all rode together a lot.

WHILE WE WERE ALMOST TOTALLY ISOLATED FROM THE REST OF THE CYCLING WORLD, WE WOULD OCCASIONALLY GET FOREIGN RIDERS IN CALIFORNIA. WE TRIED TO LEARN AS MUCH AS WE COULD FROM THEM, LITERALLY ANYTHING, FROM RACE NEWS TO RACE CRAFT OR JUST WHAT TO WEAR AND HOW TO BE MORE 'EURO'.

Larry 'The Limey' Walpole was this old British racer from East London and a real dynamo behind Belmont Bicycle Club. He had a roller racing setup that he'd built himself where the wooden drums you rode on turned a dial, so you raced head to head to get your pointer round the clock first. He was always organizing races, leading club runs and looking after new riders like me, but he was a tough teacher. He once towed me all the way to the lunch stop into a brutal head wind using a piece of fence wire wrapped round my frame to make sure I could do the whole ride. Think about that. He didn't tow me home, or let me turn round early, he towed me to the halfway point, fed me up at Peet's Cafe in Half Moon Bay, then pointed me into the tailwind home to make sure I completed the ride. That's a big lesson in sticking it out right there.

But what grabbed me most was that he had these stacks of cycling magazines from England and Europe. They were full of these stories and these illustrations and cartoons. A whole world I knew nothing about because if it wasn't on TV it didn't exist. Back then there were no videos, no internet, no other way of way of finding stuff out. Eventually I started to order books and magazines from England myself but I didn't see proper professional peloton racing until I went to the nationals in the late 1970s and it was incredible. What was really striking were these big, monstrous, powerful fields. We only had seven in our intermediates class. Even in elite in California sometimes it was just 20-30 guys in the race field as the rest would get dropped straight away.

"Larry Walpole pushes me off at the start of a 25-mile time trial"

Marcello Mugelli was an Italian racer who was over visiting family and he came down to the track to hang out with us racers. He wasn't famous but he knew about the sport and he coached me when I was about 13. He taught me track strategy, how to get rid of the other rider, how to time my sprint – a lot of that psychology you can use in all sorts of other parts of your life too. He was a cool guy. Ray Andrews was another top category road racer who came over to California from the UK and who used to drive around in a Fiat. He was this stylish British guy in an Italian car, and I couldn't imagine anyone cooler.

"Marcello taught me everything about how to race the track"

UNFORTUNATELY THAT 'SENSE OF STYLE' WAS PRETTY UNIQUE AND THE BULLYING AT SCHOOL GOT REALLY BAD AFTER ONE OF THE GIRLS FROM MY SCHOOL SAW ME OUT RIDING IN MY CYCLING GEAR. SHE WAS SAYING:

" HE HAD THESE LITTLE GIRL SOCKS ON, LITTLE BLACK SHORTS , A FUNNY SHIRT AND THIS LITTLE CAP ON "

"Fixing slot cars"

It made my life hell for at least six months afterwards though. In those days you were either a 'greaser' with duck tail hair who wanted a hot rod, or a surfer with a board who wanted a 'woodie' (station wagon). Even back in the seventh grade I thought that was just stupid and I didn't want to be either. In fact I thought the whole school scene was stupid and as a result I wasn't exactly the best student.

It didn't stop me riding though. In fact it probably made me even more determined and made my bike even more of an escape mechanism. The more I learned about the European scene the bigger the world I could escape into – at least in my head – became.

Eventually it got to the point where my mother was really worried about me. She even had me tested by the local education board and I'll always remember this guy asking me to circle how smart I was on this chart. I just thought about the grades I was getting and what most of the teachers were saying and circled 'Below average'. But then he takes that paper and this test that I'd done and he says: "NO! No. You're one of the 10 smartest kids in this whole area!" That was a real shock to me. A REAL shock. Anyway my mom put me in private school for a year straight after that and it really helped. Change of scene, people, environment, knowing that I wasn't this dumb dropout, all of that. It was really enabling and I went back to public school much stronger in my mind and myself.

AS CYCLISTS, WE WERE OUTLAWS. YOU'VE GOT TO REALIZE HOW IT WAS BACK THEN. I REMEMBER ONE TIME BEING OUT THERE RIDING, IN MY WEIRD TIGHT SHORTS AND MY LITTLE GIRL SOCKS, AND THIS POLICE PATROL CAR PULLS UP NEXT TO ME AND THE OFFICER IS TELLING ME TO GET OFF THE ROAD. HE FOLLOWED ME FOR BLOCK AFTER BLOCK AFTER BLOCK TO MAKE SURE I STAYED ON THE SIDEWALK. I WAS LITERALLY CRYING WITH FURY, THINKING THAT THIS WAS SO WRONG.

DAD   ME   MOM

In 1962 I entered my first bike race at Lake Folsom, just outside of Sacramento in California. I was only 12 but I rode in the junior 14- to 18-year-old category. I got dropped right away but I finished and by the last race of the year I was able to hang in the pack. I started racing track regularly at the Hellyer Park Velodrome around the same time. I was small, even for a junior – 5 foot 7 inches (170cm) – so I had to become an expert at sucking wheels, finding someone big, consistent and powerful and sitting behind them. I'd always try and go solo to the finish because I didn't really have a sprint but was strong on the hills. That year I was getting somewhere, regularly finishing in the top five in junior races. I was skinny so the longer the climb, the better I went. Over the next couple of years I ended up as a Class A category racer.

Being on the bike didn't just make you tough through training and racing, it was sometimes a war just being on the road. We used to regularly get attacked and run off the road, but we'd fight right back too. I remember this one time when this pick-up cut us off, screaming and yelling at us, but we caught him up at a stop light and surrounded him. We were pounding on the truck, on the windows and someone took a bike, put the chain in the little cookie and dragged the chainring teeth right across the hood. He was in the truck with his whole family and they were just cowering. Other times we'd pull people out of their cars if they pissed us off. I mean it was gnarly, man, and pretty much everyone I knew who raced or rode a bike back then was a freak.

of the Mt Hamilton road race. Walter Gimber (the well-known
_ing organizer, in the hat) is the guy who threw me out of bike racing."

"I remember this race so well. 1963 Tour of Santa Ynez Valley, Solvang. Junior race. It was the first race I didn't get dropped! On my left is Steve Lubin"

I JUST HADN'T BEEN PART OF ANY OF IT.

Long Way From Italy

Gary Fisher of Burlingame, a junior rider who competes in the all-California Road Championships Sunday near Monterey, isn't wearing a Firenze (Florence, Italy) jersey for laughs.

The 14-year-old is a member of the Belmont Bicycle Club, which has exchanged uniforms with the Florence Bicycle Club. Gary races 50 miles Sunday.

All of this hadn't stopped kids picking on me at school, but how I reacted totally changed. The first day I was back in public school this bully picked me out and fired a paper clip into my neck from real close. I just turned around and punched him straight in the nose. That was a big shock to people – and to me – but nobody ever touched me again and I actually did OK after that.

Then, in my sophomore year, we moved from Burlingame to Marin and I was a total outcast again. Looking back I was just flat out lonely but I was so used to it that I think I only really realized it when I went to the 50 year reunion recently. These people I'd been to school with were all talking about the same stories and events and I had no idea what they were going on about. I just hadn't been part of any of it.

There were some cool people at school – kids and teachers – but they were all freaks in one way or another. Mr Lamonte was the arts and crafts teacher but he was whack. He'd teach us about all sorts of wild ideas and different forms of expression and art. I spent a lot of time talking to him and an older kid called Sheldon Donig. Sheldon was a sculptor and he used to make crazy, deliberately provocative stuff like 'Pissing Dog'. He wasn't scared to be different and that made him a lot of (dangerous) fun to be around. We used to drive round in this big station wagon he had and he'd welded an I beam on the front so he could knock down walls just for fun.

Joe Brown was my metal shop teacher. He was this scary-looking dude who rode a Harley, certainly not your normal kind of teacher, but I really connected with him. He called me a 'smart cookie' in one of his lessons and those two words made an immediate and incredible difference. It was the first time any teacher had ever done that, and from then on I aced every single metalwork project. I'd always enjoyed getting hands on and creating things with my dad, who had a lot of woodworking tools. And my friend Alan Cooper's dad had a bunch of metal working tools so we'd just make stuff. Jimmy Corson was another cool guy we knew. He was into Tai Chi and eastern philosophy and he had welding torches and a kiln we could use as a forge for casting. They were the guys who really got me turned on to the whole 'making things' vibe, but I never imagined what a big part it would play in my life.

I WASN'T GOING TO CUT MY HAIR,

Outside of cycling the only group who really got us were the Hells Angels. It sounds weird because I was this skinny little kid and they were these big bike dudes, but they protected us. Our message and philosophy was so strong that they liked us, they respected us. The wheels were part of it too I guess. I can remember being on a club ride and we'd go past LSD legend Ken Kesey's house where all the Angels were hanging out. We'd see them and they'd see us and they'd just nod. We were all just freaks on the road. We were allies. We were all outsiders.

Back then if you had long hair or just looked out of the ordinary that was a really big deal. We couldn't go into certain shops and restaurants. They didn't care about the constitution, or your rights, they just weren't going to let you in. It was worse if you were a woman and far worse than that if you weren't white. It made me really angry at the time but it was actually very useful getting that understanding about being excluded, about being an outcast. Now if I'm talking to people who don't feel represented or respected I know a little bit about what they're going through. These days it looks like I was born with a total advantage. I'm 6' 2", white and with blue eyes, I have money, I look sharp and it opens things up. But I'll never forget the anger and the frustration back then when I got a lot of doors shut in my face just because I was a cyclist or because of how I looked. So I have some sense of what exclusion and discrimination feels like and that little bit of empathy can really help me connect.

I was struggling with the race scene by this time too. As I got older and I got better, things got more serious and more official. The trouble was I used to turning up with my long hair and my hippy clothes, and that started pissing the old guys off. People used to get shit just for talking to me or giving me lifts to races. Any sort of 'personality' was a problem back then but I didn't care, I thought those guys were just stupid, prejudiced and old-fashioned. Team managers saw me as a real problem, though, when they were trying make cycling look as professional as possible so people would sponsor races. They would do anything to get me disqualified, dropped or cut out and eventually the officials at the races made up some rule about my hair being too long for racing. I'm pretty sure there's never been a UCI regulation on that and I've seen this picture of me racing in Fairfax a couple of weeks before I was banned in '66, and my hair is barely over my ears.

SO I CUT THE RACING INSTEAD

That whole 'banned for long hair' thing is funny in that it comes up in almost every interview I do but it wasn't actually a big deal to me at the time. I was already getting into other stuff anyway. There was this one other kid with long hair who rode a bike too. He was the one who introduced me to the Larkspur Canyon Gang. He was like: "You ride a bike right? So do we! You gotta come and check this out." It was amazing. Larkspur Canyon and the Silver Forest redwoods are so beautiful, it was a whole other world. I mean we'd tried riding off-road on our road bikes but it was a disaster. With these ballooner bikes they had, you could get way out there. Most of the time we didn't have enough bikes so we'd have to share. Some folks would have to run and some would ride. We didn't have gears or anything either so we'd normally push more than we could pedal, but we had this whole wilderness around Mount Tamalpais to explore.

And there was nobody out there. No Sierra Club making rules and imposing restrictions on where you could go or when. No hikers, no rangers, none of that. So they started to ride off-road and explore dirt tracks. The Gang's philosophy was "No cars, no cops, no concrete" and that whole vibe was incredible. It was the next step on from just getting out on the road, because it was a real escape from everyone and everywhere else. It wasn't just the riding and freedom either. After-ride there were drum circles, parties, dancing and girls. You know it's a good gang when there are both boys and girls, especially when you're a teenager.

The whole Larkspur area was counterculture crazy too. It had been famous for parties since the Prohibition era as the hooch used to be smuggled in through Tomales Bay and then through the Canyon. That meant the first bars were in Fairfax, as that was where the good booze started. It was already a big dance and party scene and then the bohemians came in and lived out there and it was their kids I was hanging with. My ex-wife Belle's parents lived out there, with all these crazy artists and counterculture dudes, and they used to have parties that started on Friday afternoon and went on until Monday.

Ken Kesey and the Merry Pranksters crew were local to Larkspur too. They wanted to start an LSD-fueled obliteration of the entire nation, "not taken literally of course, we won't blow up their buildings, we'll blow their minds!" I never went travelling with them but I was on their bus a few times and I started up the Redwood Weed Society to mix things up at high school. I just got the other kids and said: "We need to get into the yearbook so this is what we're going to do!" That led to a whole lot of trouble but I guess it proves I've always been trying to expand people's minds, open up possibilities and improve their lives.

Because we were generally outsiders anyway there was a big crossover between the younger racers and the whole counterculture scene. Steve Lubin was the bike racer who took me to Kesey's original Acid Tests in Longshoreman's Hall. His parents owned a pharmaceutical company and they supplied Kesey and Stanford University with the acid for their experiments. You've got to remember it was still legal then. The government was actually sponsoring the experimentation with it and had been for years.

Another cyclist who was into the whole counter-culture scene was Tom Preuss, who turned the semi-clandestine Tour Del Mar road race into a public event by hiring the IDES hall and holding a dance afterwards. He hired the Quicksilver Messenger Service and the Grateful Dead to play the dance and that's the start of a whole other part of the story.

I started out like most kids. My first bike was a Schwinn Spitfire 20in wheeler, the classic 'under the Christmas tree' present with training wheels and mudguards. Then I got a Raleigh Colt 26in wheeled roadster. It had a three-speed Sturmey-Archer rear hub. The seat tube was a little bit shorter and the top tube curved at the back end like a fastback design so you could really drop the saddle. It certainly wasn't a race bike though as it had these big swept butterfly handlebars in a zero reach stem.

With such a tiny riding scene, finding decent bikes wasn't easy. There was only one American 'racing bike' – The Schwinn Paramount – but everyone wanted a real European bike. The only good cycle shop was American Cyclery on Frederick Street in San Francisco. That had been around since 1941 and was run by Oscar Juner, who'd been a professional track racer in the '30s and '40s. Peter Rich then set up Velosport Berkeley in '62. He was a local racer and they were a real big supporter of the local scene. They even had a place to stay above the shop if you were a racer from out of town or you had nowhere else to live.

By 14 I was working in my local bike shop. The owner, Larry Elsworth, was my first business teacher. I was only a kid but he always made sure I looked super-smart with a proper Schwinn dealer mechanic outfit and pocket protectors and everything. I worked there three years, starting just sweeping up, cleaning, and fixing punctures, but I soon started wrenching and I learned fast.

That meant my first 'proper' bike was a Legnano. Legnano was a mass market Italian brand designed for the US but it still had a decent Columbus steel frame, which was the gold standard back then. It had Italian Campagnolo gears too and, within the first week of owning it, I found a kid who was prepared to swap his glue-on tubular tires and wheels for my heavy clincher wheels and tires. So I had proper race wheels with Campagnolo hubs on Fiamme red label rims, just like the racers used.

My first custom bike was something really special. At that time there were only two custom builders in the whole US – a guy in Chicago and Lars Zabroskie in California. Lars was this really cool guy with cool shades, a cool girlfriend, a cool house and this souped-up minibus which he used to drive like a lunatic. His brand was Paragon and he built a super-light bike for me. I guess my grandpa's obsessive technical side had rubbed off on me, and it was definitely a sign of things to come, because that bike was built exactly how I wanted. And because I was a skinny climber what I wanted was to save weight anywhere I could. That meant it was a complete mix of the lightest possible components. It had no Campagnolo parts, which was shocking at the time. Instead I had these partially plastic Simplex mechs and TA cotter pin cranks. I even had it built to take Mafac cyclo-cross cantilever brakes rather than heavier sidepull brakes, which really offended some people. It was a proper one-off and I loved it.

I've always thought that it's dumb when nonconformist groups have a uniform and I've always had a strong and independent idea about image. That started with cycling I guess, scavenging together my own version of what I saw the European racers wearing in magazines. Those little white girl's gym socks got me into a load of trouble at school, but I looked right on the bike and that was what mattered.

THE LARKSPUR
CANYON GANG
MADE ME REALIZE
I WASN'T THE ONLY
WILD ONE OUT THERE,
COS WE WERE ALL OUTCASTS,
AND THEY HOOKED
ME UP
WITH SOME OF THE CRAZIEST
YEARS HUMANITY
HAD SEEN.

BICYCLE RACE
and FOLK-ROCK FESTIVAL

PESCADERO, CALIFORNIA   AUGUST 26 – 27 – 28

* FRIDAY –   FOLK-ROCK DANCE
  8:00 P.M.
  IDES Hall, Pescadero, Calif.

* SATURDAY – OLYMPIC DEVELOPMENT BICYCLE RACE
  9:00 A.M. to 3:00 P.M.
  Folk Rock Music – 12:00 to 5:00 P.M.
  Dance – 8:00 P.M., IDES Hall

* SUNDAY –   MORE BICYCLE RACES
  9:00 to 3:00 P.M.
  Folk Rock Music – 12:00 to 3:00 P.M.
  Dance – 8:00 P.M., IDES Hall

TRIP ON OUT TO THE HAPPENINGS AND DIG THE ACTION!

FEATURING

QUICK SILVER MESSENGER SERVICE
RECORDING STARS

GRATEFUL DEAD
TV & RECORDING STARS

COLLOSAL POMEGRANATE
LOCAL &
NATIONAL STARS

AUGUST 26, 27, 28'
PESCADERO,
CALIFORNIA

I JUST STARTED HANGING OUT MORE AND GOING HOME LESS AND THAT WAS IT, THAT WAS THE START OF THE NEW ADVENTURE.

We were already doing some wild things with the Larkspur Canyon Gang. When my fellow rider Steve Lubin took me to the Longshoremen's Hall for the Trips Festival that was part of the Acid Tests, I was only 15. That was in January '66 and it was in July that year when I first met the Grateful Dead. Tom Preuss had hired them to play a party at the finish of the previously semi-clandestine Tour Del Mar. The race ran over a weekend but, as a publicity stunt, Tom and some other guys set up this parade 'stage' on the Friday. We went from the Ferry Building in San Francisco, picking up keys to the cities we passed through from the mayors of each place. The parade even went to the Playboy Club en route so they could get promotional pictures with the Bunny Girls, but I was too young to get in there.

The Grateful Dead and Quicksilver Messenger Service were riding in Cadillacs within the peloton. We all rolled into town to finish at the IDES Hall, which was where the bands were going to play. So I'm there while they're setting up and Girl Freiberg, the wife of David from the Quick Silver Messenger Service, just takes me by the hand and leads me out into the meadow in the back and we start making out. We all stayed at the same hotel in Pescadero that weekend and just hung out. I mean I was this geeky little 15-year-old kid and suddenly this is all happening to me and it's crazy.

To be honest when I first heard the Grateful Dead I thought that they sounded terrible, as their sound system was really bad but the scene around them was fascinating. I just started hanging out more and going home less and that was it, that was the start of the new adventure. My mom didn't like that at all. Thanks to my grandpa and the movies, she'd seen enough showbiz types in her life already.

It was an intense time with crazy stuff going on – the Vietnam War, the rise of environmentalism, civil disobedience, riots – and the scene was a response to this insanity. That's what the whole Merry Prankster, Acid Tests thing was about – saying we can't go on like this and looking for ways to create something better, something more beautiful.

The straights just didn't understand what was going on. For us "tune in, turn on, drop out" wasn't about getting wasted and forgetting what was happening, it was about totally opening our minds so we could create incredible things. Back then LSD, or acid, was legal – it was only made illegal in California in October 1966. People like the psychologist Timothy Leary and the Beatniks had been experimenting with it for years, but it was actually within a really small group of people. Then Ken Kesey and the Pranksters set off on this cross-country mission in this crazily-painted school bus to spread the message everywhere. They called the bus "Furthur" [sic] because that was where they always said they were heading. Then Bear (Augustus Owlsey Stanley) started mass producing LSD and the Acid Tests started.

The Acid Tests were really just big parties where everyone would be on acid because they'd mix it into Kool-Aid, that's where that saying "Have you drunk the Kool-Aid?" originally comes from! (10 years later it would, sadly, become associated with the Jonestown massacre). Another saying at the time was, "We gotta dose that guy" because we knew you had to be careful with how much each person got. You had to have someone there to help you in and out. You'd always have people with you, especially if you were using it for the first time, because everyone would react so differently. The Acid Tests were exactly that – tests of where you could go, how far your mind could expand when you used it. The environments had to be really controlled too. Timothy Leary always used to talk about "set and setting". In other words, you had to come in with the right, open and curious mindset but you also had to be in a really positive, enabling and safe social and physical setting.

The music was part of it but when I started going to see the Grateful Dead they sounded like shit and there were like maybe 100 people there, including the crew. It was the 'setting' rather than the music that fascinated me at first, the soundscape and the visuals, creating and controlling that whole environment. I guess it was a throwback to the stories my grandpa told about making movies talk and getting the sound right in theaters to create a complete immersion in the experience. Those parties my parents used to throw and my dad's abstract impressionism stuff certainly came in too.

I started getting into lighting the shows first, making the communication visual as well as sonic. There was a real practical science to that which really appealed to me. It was all about taking the available equipment, making it work in totally different ways and combining different pieces together. Nothing we used was stock, we modified and boosted everything. We'd use army surplus gear to increase the horsepower of the lights, the projectors, the power sources. I made this electrical base board that you could connect direct to the grid with alligator clips and it would give you 160 amps of power even down 100 yards of cable. So we'd just find the nearest power line, shin up the poles and hook in. We'd use DC motors so we could change the speed and direction of the color wheels. Multiple wheels and clock faces on microphone booms meant we had this incredible interplay of images and effects on the screen.

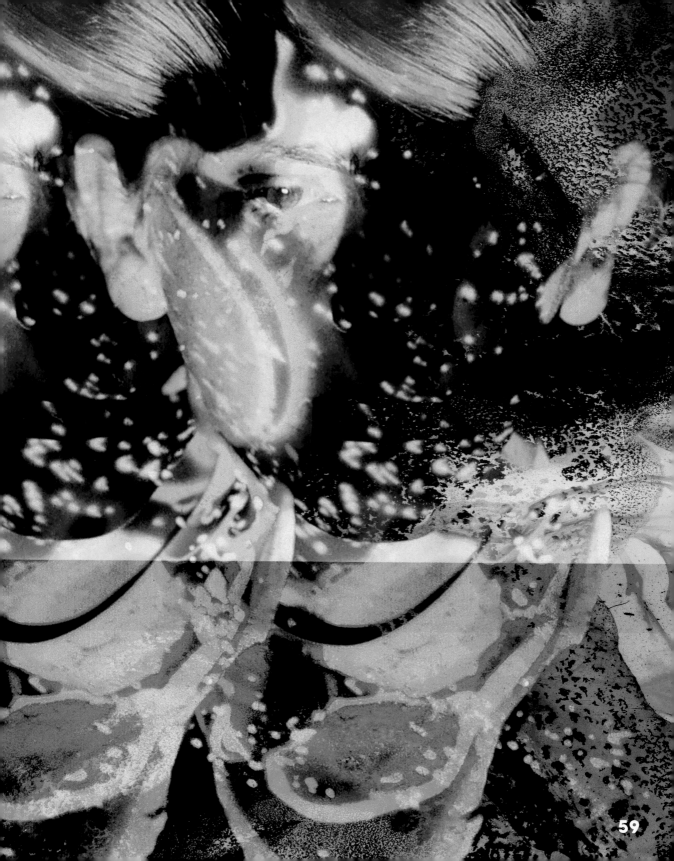

We were constantly experimenting with the oils, liquids and gels on the slides. We had these incredible oils that were super-vibrant but absolutely transparent; you could look through a bottle of the oil but a couple of drops on a slide gave this really dark pigment. There was a lot of science involved in finding out what would mix with what to produce the results we needed, but we also really pushed the images. We produced these films where we painted this naked girl in all these incredible colors and she was dancing and we'd loop that and multiply it. She was beautiful, man, and people would go crazy.

We took what we were doing really seriously, though. That was the attitude, using industrial means and techniques to create these incredible environments. Rigging the projectors, the screens, trying to get them up onto walls using banqueting tables and furniture because we didn't have any scaffolding. Getting the best quality screens we could, making the venues as dark as possible so the contrast was as high as possible, using backlit setups so the whole rig was hidden behind the screen. Man, it was hard work, real science and engineering.

It was expensive too. We built the light show totally from scratch and my main partner in crime was Alan Cooper. He was a really smart guy and went on to be pretty famous in the computer business for inventing Visual Basic and a bunch of other really practical innovations. We used to ask for $1,000 for a show, but Bill Graham, who was the promoter for most of the shows, only wanted to pay us $100. That wouldn't even cover the bulbs we blew in one night!

We had a loft in a warehouse in Sausalito where we built a practice space to build and try out the gear. We used wood from a whisky distillery to make some of it, so it smelled incredible. Then I built an inflatable cube for the light show tests. It was 20 x 20 x 10 feet high and I built that thing for just $20 with 12-foot rolls of plastic sheeting held together with vinyl tape and one tiny attic fan. The cube had one white side and the others were black and we had it tethered out in the woods with rope so we could practice projecting the light shows. It was out in West Marin near a place called Forest Knowles and there was a swimming pool out there, so I got a water heater and a pump and I used that to heat up the pool so we could swim in it. I was still like 16, 17 years old, and when you think of the technology today it's like night and day. But man we did some cool stuff and the light show became a massive part of the whole experience.

also used to work with Bear on the sound. Again it was all about the quality and the clarity. There's no point just being loud; you have to have really high quality sound so you still get that intense experience half a mile away, otherwise it's just noise. The whole attitude and theory of the sound development was having something that could be as big as Woodstock but still super-high quality. Bear was the guy who created the 'Wall of Sound', this incredible bank of custom speakers that you could hear from a mile away and it would still be a clear, clean sound. He was the guy who started taping two microphones together to stop the feedback, using stage monitors so the band could hear how they sounded, recording live albums from behind the mixing desk so they actually sounded good. He was a genius at it and he ended up doing sound for Janis Joplin, Jimi Hendrix, Jefferson Airplane, Santana, Johnny Cash, and so many people.

He was someone who a lot of people would have seen as just another hippy on a trip. Actually he was this totally creative and driven dude who didn't see any barriers to taking what he'd created all around the world.

That didn't just apply to the sound shows. Bear also used to make industrial quantities of LSD. He made over 500g between 1965 and 1967, five million doses! He used to give it out to a lot to bands – he allegedly supplied The Beatles with LSD when they were filming *Magical Mystery Tour* – and for free to other people to grow the scene. He also used it to buy equipment and to help out the band. But he made a ton of money as well. The LA Times actually ran a story about him with the headline "LSD Millionaire" the day before they criminalized it in California. The Grateful Dead wrote a song about that and called it 'Alice D. Millionaire'.

There were other really inspirational people in the scene. John Barlow was a writer for the Dead but he went on to set up the Electronic Frontier Foundation, designed to protect internet civil liberties. One of his EFF co-founders was John Gilmore, who developed what evolved into the DHCP computer address protocol which governs the way computers communicate online. Painters, artists, musicians; that short time really opened and changed some very important minds and so many things have happened because of that.

EVEN APPLE CO-FOUNDER STEVE JOBS TALKED ABOUT THOSE TIMES AND HOW THEY CHANGED THE WAY PEOPLE THOUGHT: NOT FOLLOWING CONVENTION, STARTING WITH A FRESH SHEET OF HOW THINGS SHOULD WORK RATHER THAN HOW THEY WORKED ALREADY.

There were no boundaries to doing what you wanted, whoever you were and however old you were. If you had an idea, then just go out and make it happen. That's how we started taking care of the environments outside the concerts too. Jimmy Corson, his partner Annie and I became GUSS (Grand Ultimate Stewardship Services). We used to take care of the rock 'n' rollers at the before and after parties and arranged anything else they wanted or needed. We started cooking for parties and they became banquets and so we started making the furniture and fittings for them. We made everything. They knew we could be trusted to do something really special. If there was a band coming into town to play and they wanted something making or a party organizing we were the ones doing it. I see pictures now of the scene and I see our stuff everywhere. It's cool, it's like: "Hey, look, they're sitting at that table we made!"

We even did the gardening and decorating for some of the band's houses. Jefferson Airplane had this exquisite Victorian mansion on Fulton Street in San Fransisco that we decorated for them. It was really beautiful with all the original features so we did a really respectful job with that. We cleaned it up, lit it really well and we filled it with our furniture. We decorated every room differently, but it was complementary and it was beautiful, man. The original Grateful Dead houses in Ashbury were more crazy. We painted them in these mad colors, walls were removed and other walls were added.

"Grateful Dead founder member Ron 'Pigpen' McKernan outside 710 Ashbury Street. It was a communal living space – I lived there too for a while"

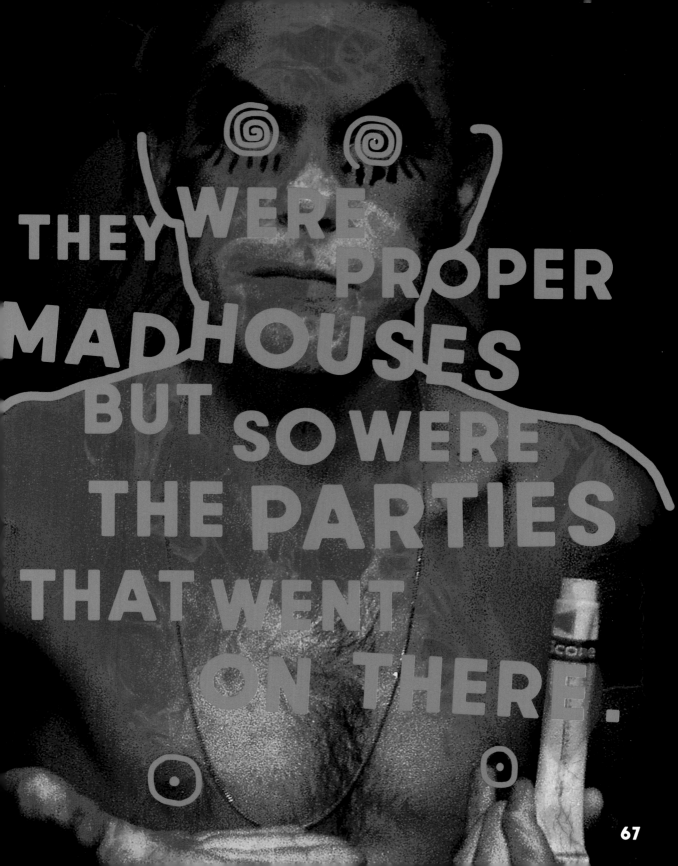

THEY WERE PROPER MADHOUSES BUT SO WERE THE PARTIES THAT WENT ON THERE.

67

Steve Miller Band
Kalidascope
YoungBloods
♥ MAY ♥
10 · 11 · 12
Carousel
Ballroom
Van Hess and Market

It wasn't the 'hippy scene' that people think of now, that was just a lazy uniform that was meant to look different but everyone ended up looking the same. The way I dressed, what I did, I wanted to have a look, and I loved creating my own style. We weren't going to be straight – not even the band managers wore suits – and we weren't gonna be 'scruffians' either. That what was what we called the hippy kids on the street who just did the drugs but didn't get the scene.

We started putting shows and parties on in this amazing venue called the Carousel Ballroom and we became known as the Carousellians. It was a really good venue and we would lay on really good food, really good wine. Not just expensive but real whole earth, healthy, natural, wonderful food just like how my grandpa Fred had raised me. We'd polish these amazing dance floors, we made these proper seats and furniture, and we had the lighting and the sound totally dialed.

The scene was starting to turn into a nightmare though. Tom Wolfe had brought out *The Electric Kool-Aid Acid Test,* his book about Kesey, the Pranksters and Furthur. *Fear and Loathing in Las Vegas* would come out a few years later and everyone was just focused on this sex and drugs and rock and roll media hype. That Scott McKenzie song – "If you're going to San Francisco, be sure to wear some flowers in your hair" – was number one most places in the world in the summer of '67 and suddenly everyone was heading to California to get laid and get high. That song was just released to promote the Monterey Pop Festival, which McKenzie's label had set up. Even Frank Zappa joked about it. The Mothers of Invention, the band he helmed, called their 1968 album 'We're Only In It for The Money'. One of the tracks – *Who Needs the Peace Corps* – includes the line "I'll go to Frisco, buy a wig and sleep on Owsley's floor".

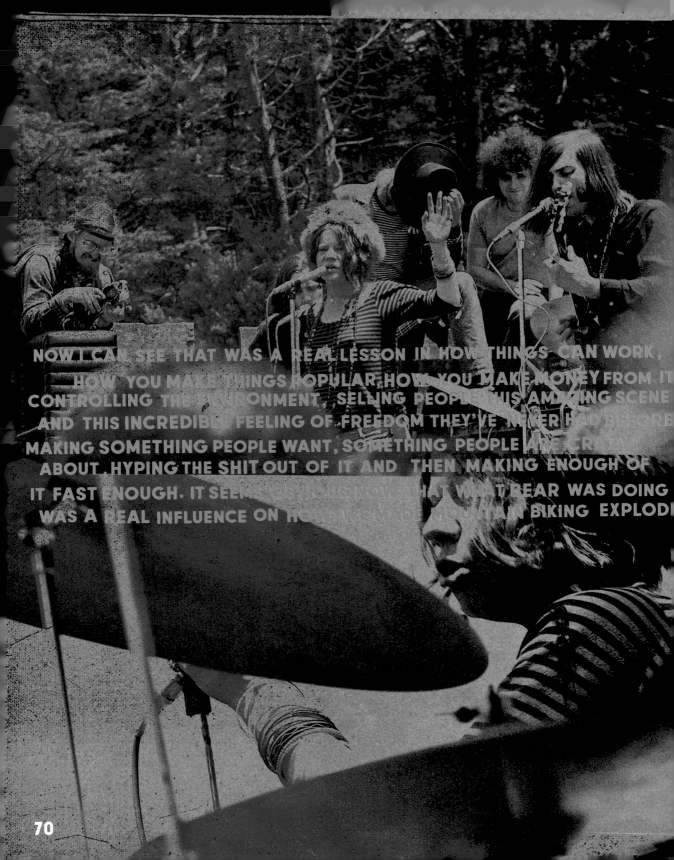

NOW I CAN SEE THAT WAS A REAL LESSON IN HOW THINGS CAN WORK, HOW YOU MAKE THINGS POPULAR, HOW YOU MAKE MONEY FROM IT, CONTROLLING THE ENVIRONMENT, SELLING PEOPLE THIS AMAZING SCENE AND THIS INCREDIBLE FEELING OF FREEDOM THEY'VE NEVER HAD BEFORE, MAKING SOMETHING PEOPLE WANT, SOMETHING PEOPLE ARE CRAZY ABOUT, HYPING THE SHIT OUT OF IT AND THEN MAKING ENOUGH OF IT FAST ENOUGH. IT SEEMS OBVIOUS NOW THAT WHAT BEAR WAS DOING WAS A REAL INFLUENCE ON HOW WE MADE MOUNTAIN BIKING EXPLODE

I guess all that was cool in some ways because it spread the whole anti-war movement, flower power, thinking about the planet, the idea of being free of convention all around the world, but all these people coming in attracted the wrong sort of attention. The drug dealers saw it as open season. They were coming in with cocaine, and that really changed things for the worse. They would say it wasn't addictive but we used to say: "Coke makes a new man out of you, but the new man wants a hit too." It was bad shit but these kids didn't know anything so they took whatever was sold to them. Meth, coke, whatever, they were just out to get high. Not to free their minds so they could create, develop and expand themselves, which is why we did it. We didn't even smoke weed or drink when taking LSD because we wanted to control the experience, but they just wanted to get wasted. The scene used to be about communication but I can remember Owsley saying: "This is bad shit, this is like taking all the files in your head and just throwing them on the floor." When the coke came in, money started coming in too and the whole scene changed.

The dealers weren't just selling drugs either, they wanted a take on anything making money. I would go out to sell tickets for the Carousel and then the dealers started wanting all those tickets. It was heavy, man, I was having guns put in my face, it was getting real dark. Even though the Carousel was this incredible place it wasn't making any money. If you look it up on Wikipedia it says that the six months we ran it were "a social/musical laboratory experiment" and that's right. We were about the experience and we were so into it we didn't even think about the business side. We certainly never made a profit from the shows as we were always buying new gear. The bulbs we were using cost around $100 each and we would blow several every time!

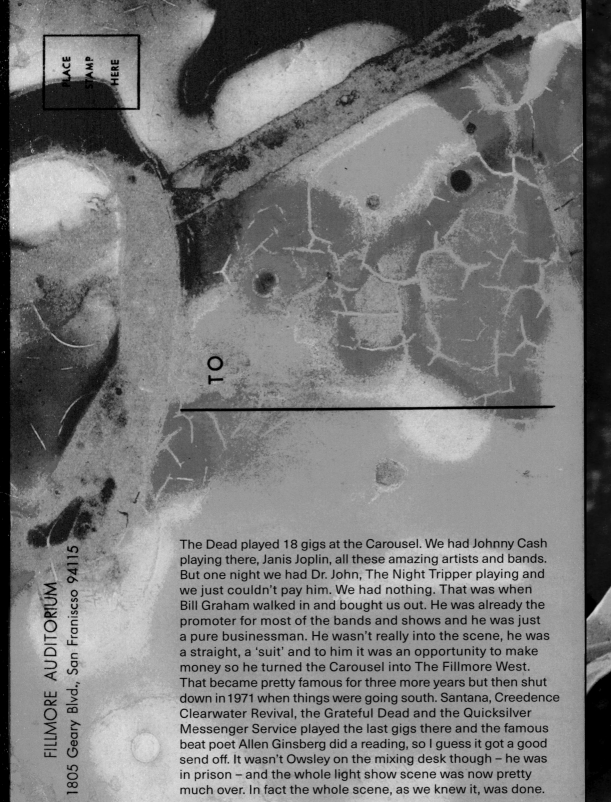

TO

_____

FILLMORE AUDITORIUM
1805 Geary Blvd., San Franiscso 94115

The Dead played 18 gigs at the Carousel. We had Johnny Cash
playing there, Janis Joplin, all these amazing artists and bands.
But one night we had Dr. John, The Night Tripper playing and
we just couldn't pay him. We had nothing. That was when
Bill Graham walked in and bought us out. He was already the
promoter for most of the bands and shows and he was just
a pure businessman. He wasn't really into the scene, he was
a straight, a 'suit' and to him it was an opportunity to make
money so he turned the Carousel into The Fillmore West.
That became pretty famous for three more years but then shut
down in 1971 when things were going south. Santana, Creedence
Clearwater Revival, the Grateful Dead and the Quicksilver
Messenger Service played the last gigs there and the famous
beat poet Allen Ginsberg did a reading, so I guess it got a good
send off. It wasn't Owsley on the mixing desk though – he was
in prison – and the whole light show scene was now pretty
much over. In fact the whole scene, as we knew it, was done.

The Altamont Speedway Free Festival on December 6 1969 was the real death blow. It was always going to be a disaster. The idea was to have this Woodstock in the West, a free concert headlined by the Rolling Stones and the Grateful Dead in Golden Gate Park in San Francisco. But shortly before the date the city and the Police Department shut that idea down. There was talk of moving it to Sears Point Raceway, but its owners wanted a massive payment as the Stones would be filming it. That's why, at the last moment, it ended up in Altamont. There was no time to set things up properly and there was no crowd control. People were just wandering everywhere backstage, there were drugs and groupies every-where, and though the Hells Angels were on security they'd been drinking all day and they were losing control. Fights were breaking out, the Angels were tooled up with chains and snooker cues and trying to push people back, but the lead singer of a local band who was six months pregnant had her skull fractured by a beer bottle thrown from the crowd. One of the guys from Jefferson Airplane jumped off stage during their set to try to sort out another problem and a Hells Angel knocked him cold. Jerry Garcia and the Dead heard about that and they just left straight away, didn't even play.

Mick Jagger had already been punched in the head by one of the crowd as he got out of his helicopter and then when they came on stage this guy called Meredith Hunter tried to get on stage too. The story is that his girlfriend had a crush on Jagger and Hunter was out to get him, they pushed him back a couple of times but he was crazy, off his head. He fights his way back to the front and suddenly he pulls a gun to try and shoot Jagger, one of the Angels sees him, knocks the pistol out of the way and then stabs him to death. We didn't even know what had happened on the stage, it was totally out of control. Another couple of people died when someone drove a car through the crowd. Somebody else died in a drainage ditch after getting too high. The whole neighborhood was trashed, it was horrific man, it was a war zone, just horrible to see. We knew right then that it was over.

Predictably Altamont made the authorities even more against the whole scene. You've already got all these civil rights and anti-war protests going on and they were cracking down hard. I can remember Janis Joplin playing at the Carousel and the police tactical squad were outside with batons and helmets and we had the Hells Angels on security and it was tense, man. Bear got arrested that night and he ended up being inside for five years. The Grateful Dead and most of the crew got busted in New Orleans soon after. I had a really bad trip and ended up spending a night in the juve cube – juvenile custody – and that was not a good place to be in that state.

The Dead and other bands had got successful enough to have their own homes so we weren't all hanging out together in the commune anymore either.

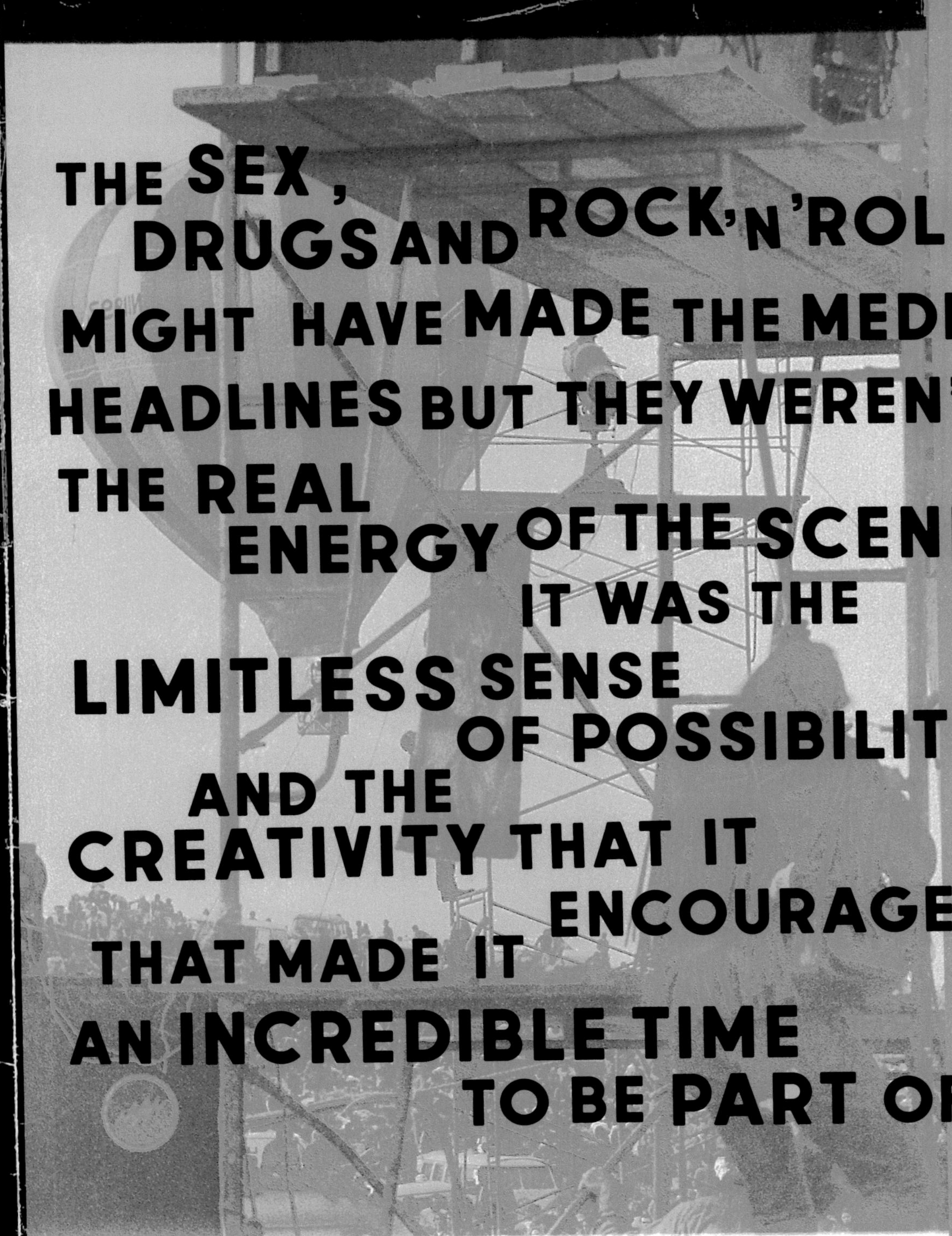

THE SEX ,
   DRUGS AND ROCK'N'ROLL
MIGHT HAVE MADE THE MEDIA
HEADLINES BUT THEY WEREN'T
THE REAL
        ENERGY OF THE SCENE.
                  IT WAS THE
   LIMITLESS SENSE
           OF POSSIBILITY
      AND THE
CREATIVITY THAT IT
              ENCOURAGED
   THAT MADE IT
AN INCREDIBLE TIME
           TO BE PART OF .

It had been an amazing time with incredible people doing awesome things but it was done. I remember going out for a 10-mile ride and I had to sleep for the rest of the day. That told me something. It told me it was time for a new chapter, a new adventure. Thankfully I knew where to find it.

WE WEREN'T THE SAME AS THE OTHERS.
WE DIDN'T THINK THE SAME
AND WE DIDN'T WANT TO LOOK THE SAME EITHER.

The scene was a great time to experiment with clothes. We weren't the same as the others. We didn't think the same and we didn't want to look the same either. There was definitely a hippy 'look', but the original culture was about celebrating yourself and how you saw yourself as an individual. My original look was influenced by a band called The Charlatans and was a contemporary take on classic Western. Not the full cowboy look but more the business look from that time, the kind of thing my great-grandad would have worn. It made us stand out when we were the Carousellians.

WITH THESE FAT
BALLOON TIRES,
WE HAD THIS INCREDIBLE
GOLDEN KEY
TO GO WILD AND GET LOST.
IT WAS BACK TO THAT MANTRA OF
"NO CARS,
NO COPS,
NO CONCRETE"
AND NOT MANY CARES
ABOUT ANYTHING ELSE.

"Berry Allen and me fixing up the metro truck – I painted it blue eventually and it took us everywhere, from light shows to bike races. I even came back from a trip to France in 1979 to find someone living in it"

WHEN I LEFT THE SCENE I WAS IN A BAD SHAPE PHYSICALLY AND PROBABLY MENTALLY TOO, BUT I WAS YOUNG AND IT DIDN'T TAKE LONG TO START TO FEEL REALLY ALIVE, STRONGER AND READY TO START ROAD RACING AGAIN.

After the deaths and disaster at the Altamont Festival, the Carousel being taken over and the commune dispersing as the Grateful Dead became more successful, the scene that I once loved had come apart. Cocaine was a big problem too. All of a sudden things went from consciousness expansion and an elegant, advanced way of life to dealers with guns, and people crashing into the scene talking shit, and girls getting under tables for a line of coke. I didn't want to be any part of that and, in contrast, cycling seemed so clean.

When I left the scene I was in a bad shape physically and probably mentally too, but I was young and it didn't take long to start to feel really alive, stronger and ready to start road racing again. I'd grown five inches since I'd quit as a junior and I started working hard and I became the breakaway guy. I could line races out 32-34mph for two or three minutes until the group just came apart. I was determined too. Nobody was going to drop me and I made sure they knew that nobody drops me.

I used to travel all over. I still had the big light show van but I used to ride my bike to the airport to fly to races too. I can remember riding from LAX through some rough neighborhoods to a race in Los Angeles and these dudes were like: "Hey! Let me take a look at that bicycle. That looks real expensive." I just had to sprint the hell out of there but I got to that race pretty warmed up!

Man, that rush you get from putting in 400-mile weeks and slowly becoming a superman. The whole physicality of it. Getting the most from your body and mind. Really pushing them to see what they can do is really important mentally. I like that you have to earn it too. A lot of people see cyclists, mountain bikers, whoever, riding up hills, straining, sweating and they think, that looks slow and painful, that guy must be miserable. And yeah, sometimes it does really hurt, but the feeling of power it gives you is incredible. That sensation you get after four hard weeks when your body is really starting to respond, growing stronger, getting leaner.

That feeling is incredible and I need it now as much as I did back then. It creates a really strong shared experience too, really connects you with those who understand. I remember talking to Jens Voigt, the legendary strong man road racer, about making solo breaks. He said: "You go this pace, this pace, this pace, and then when they start chasing hard you go THAT pace." That's exactly it, that thrill of the hunt, evading the chase, going out there against everyone, putting everything on the line. Man that feeling is incredible even now I'm 70 and I just get eaten. They always stick me in the front row at events these days because I'm a 'celebrity' but I get passed by like 40 riders in the first lap, even on a short CX course, it's just funny. Anyway back then I was strong.

MY RACING STARTS WERE GREAT
SO I COULD ALWAYS GET THE
HOLESHOT AND THAT'S JUST SUCH
AN AWESOME FEELING,
IT'S ANOTHER
SORT OF TRIP,
BUT JUST
AS ADDICTIVE.

MARINITE IN THE LEAD
Gary Fisher of Marin's Velo-Club Tamalpais led through a turn during the criterium race of the Tour of Marin Sunday in Fairfax. Bill Handsan of Sacramento took the event, while Keith Vierra of Palo Alto was the overall winner.

(Photo by Michael Silberberg)

WITH THESE FAT BALLOON TIRES, WE HAD THIS INCREDIBLE GOLDEN KEY TO GO AND GET LOST, IT WAS AWESOME.

It wasn't just road racing that was getting me back onto the bike and feeling great again. As soon as I split the scene and headed back to Marin County I got back in touch with the Larkspur Gang.

I WENT ON A COUPLE OF RIDES WITH THEM AND SUDDENLY I STARTED LAUGHING AGAIN. IT WAS JUST HILARIOUS, NOBODY WAS TAKING IT SERIOUSLY. 80% OF THE TIME YOU WERE PUSHING, TALKING, GOOFING AROUND, BUT THEN THAT 20% OF THE TIME WHEN YOU WERE CHARGING BACK DOWN THE MOUNTAIN IT WAS A TOTAL BLAST. THIS WAS BEFORE ANYONE IN MARIN STARTED MODIFYING STUFF. WE WERE JUST RIDING BIKES WE FOUND UNTIL THEY BROKE OR FELL APART. YOU'D GO OUT WITH SIX OF YOU AND AT LEAST THREE OF THE BIKES WOULD BE DRAGGED BACK HOME BECAUSE THEY WERE BROKEN. THAT WAS STILL WAY BETTER THAN RIDING A CYCLO-CROSS BIKE PROPERLY OFF ROAD THOUGH AS THEN YOU HAD TO SPEND THREE HOURS PATCHING PUNCTURES AFTERWARDS, SO IT WAS JUST A NON-STARTER.

It was awesome. We could get way out there into the Silver Forest and Mount Tamalpais and back again in two to three hours, or we'd just stay out there all day exploring.

I met back up with my schoolfriend Sheldon Donig when I went back to Marin too. He was the crazy sculptor who used to drive the car with the metal beam on the front for demolishing stuff. Except now he was into owning buildings instead and he hooked me up with a room in one of his places. I was the only guy in a house with three girls around my age. They were all beautiful and one of them wrote porn stories. That was an awesome place to live for a while and luck sure does play a big part in life. But it turned out they were all horny as hell too, so I had to get out of there pretty quick before they killed me.

The next place I rented was a shack. That's what the landlord actually called it. A shack. 69 Mono Lane, Fairfax was the address and the actor W.C. Fields had rented it in the 1930s. It was actually an old speakeasy that was still a bar and liquor store, where I used to work. In summer there was no air conditioning so we used to sit in the walk-in freezer looking out of the door for customers. There was no door on the toilet either so you had to open the freezer door across the gap to give you some privacy. That's what the girls did when they came round. If we were really hungry we used to go to over to the Deer Park Inn for a prime rib that we'd bring home in a cardboard box and eat in the store.

That's when I met Charlie Kelly. People kept saying: "You gotta meet this guy Charlie, he's just like you, he's crazy about bikes!" And sure enough when I met him he had an orange Colnago road race bike almost exactly the same as mine and we hit it off straight away. He had a place over a recording studio and he needed a roommate to share it with, so I moved in – it was perfect. Jimmy's No Problem Cafe was right next door to the apartment and was one of the two places in the whole area where you could get a decent espresso – so it was the perfect spot for meeting other riders.

There were some great guys riding too. Jobst Brandt was a fascinating character. He was an engineer and he had worked at Porsche, Hewlett Packard, Avocet bike computers and on nuclear physics with the Stanford Linear Accelerator Center – a real genius. He would always be able to tell you how stuff was made and why. Especially bike details such as the slight scoop on the surface of tapered crank axles that let the crank expand under pressure so the corners fit tighter than they would if the axles were flat. All the really geeky stuff that fascinated me fascinated him too. Brandt's book *The Bicycle Wheel* turned some of the traditional 'facts' about wheelbuilding on their head too.

Jobst was mostly a really hard rider. He used to put on these epic self-supported, minimal kit rides out into the Sierras. Back then I rode a five-speed block with a 20-tooth cog at the top end and some of the passes he found had pitches of around 27% so things got pretty brutal.

"YOU GOTTA MEET THIS GUY CHARLIE, HE'S JUST LIKE YOU, HE'S CRAZY ABOUT BIKES!"

John Finley Scott was another guy who I rode with back then. He was a professor and an engineer and, in 1953, he'd converted a Schwinn World frame with derailleur gears and cantilever brakes to create what he called a 'woodsie' bike. He was a really big influence on me. If you ever talked shit about anything he would call you out and slam you down hard, but I learned a lot that way. John was also one of the first people to invest in MountainBikes. He loaned us $10,000. I'm jumping ahead again though. Back then it was the riding and the feeling I belonged to a really interesting, smart scene with people who thought differently to the squares but thought the same as me that was the big deal.

JOBST USED TO TAKE US OVER LOT OF ROUGH TRACKS AND RIGHT OUT INTO THE MIDDLE OF NOWHERE TOO . IF HE TOLD YOU TO BRING TWO TIRES TO COPE WITH PUNCTURES YOU KNEW YOU WERE GOING TO BE OUT THERE A LONG TIME AND IT WAS GOING TO BE TOUGH .

ALLAN M. HANSON
President / Publisher

WILLIAM PARK
Business Manager

GAIL ELLEN HEILMAN
Editor

ANNETTE THOMPSON
Art Director

FRED DE LONG
Technical Editor

**RICHARD JOW
GARY FISHER
BILL MC CREADY**
Associate Editors

DARRYL SKRABAK
Legislative Editor

GARY J. HAWKINS
European Correspondent

**OWEN MULHOLLAND
FRANK BERTO
EUGENE GASTON, M.D.
DAVID L. SMITH, M.D.**
Contributing Editors

HELEN EPPERSON
Copy Editor

WARD CLEAVELAND
Circulation Director

TERESA SAM
Circulation Manager

PUBLICATIONS

Advertising/Marketing
WILMA BRIGHAM
119 Paul Drive, P.O. Box 4450, San
Rafael, Calif. 94903

East & Midwest, **WILLIAM
FIELDS, III,** Specifax Media Sales,
22 Montgomery St., Boston, Mass.
02216; (617) 262-7532

Texas, **BILL FIELDS,** 5435 Ells-
worth Ave., Dallas, Texas 75206;
(214) 826-7860

BICYCLING! is published monthly by **Capital
Management Publications,** 119 Paul Drive,
P.O. Box 4450, San Rafael, CA 94903. Phone
(415) 472-4711. Subscription rate: United States
and Canada, $9.50 per year; all other countries,
$11.50. Single copy price, $1.00. Second-class
postage paid at San Rafael, California and at
additional mailing offices. Copyright by Capital
Management Publication, 1976. **Send Form
3579 to Bicycling!,** P.O. Box 4450, San Rafael,
CA 94903.
EDITORIAL contributions about touring,
equipment, accessories, repairs, health, racing
and safety are welcome. All must be accompa-
nied by a self-addressed stamped envelope.
Capital Management Publications assumes no
responsibility for loss or damage of submitted
material. Submission of the manuscript, which
includes all sketches, drawings, photos and
other art work, to Bicycling! Magazine is the
author's warranty that the material is in no way
an infringement upon the rights of others and
that the material is released for publication
without additional approval.

ON THE COVER:
If you go prepared for a little
rain, a little mist, you'll enjoy
every moment of your tour of
England and Scotland. Our
special feature starts on page
34. Photo by Frank Krygowski.

BICYCLING!

January 1977 — Vol. XVIII, No. 1

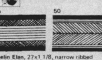

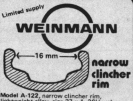

Those mid-70s years were such great times. I was properly fit again and working for *Bicycling* magazi getting free test kit to use as well as earning a few hundred bucks a month in winnings from racing on the road with our team. In between I'd work in the liquor store and help Charlie with his moving busin He'd do house removals, office relocations and such but his specialty was moving pianos. Pianos are nightmare. Really heavy and really delicate, so you need someone you can really trust and know really w I even had a job selling Christmas trees from a plantation one winter – that was my mother's idea to g me back on the straight and narrow. But through all this there was one thing taking up more and more my thinking time: creating the perfect off-road bike.

Because the more I rode off-road, the more I saw how to make my bike better. Lighter and easier to climb on so I didn't have to push as much. Stronger and more controlled to survive the descents off Mount Tamalpais and the other places we were riding.

IT WASN'T ROCKET SCIENCE BUT WHAT REALLY EXCITED ME WAS THAT OFF-ROAD BIKES WERE A TOTALLY BLANK CANVAS. THERE WERE NO LIMITS OR STANDARDS OR TRADITIONS. JUST POSSIBILITIES.

In contrast, road race bikes were basically a standard issue object and they had been for decades. The were all basically identical. There was no real difference year to year, so the only way you could age fram was by looking at the serial number. You either had Columbus or Reynolds tubes but the frames and handlir geometry were nearly all the same apart from fractions of inches and degrees. Everyone in the world, besides perhaps the French, were riding Campagnolo equipment. At the Davis Double Century, a 200-mi bike ride in the Yolo, Napa and Lake areas of California, Jobst used to hand out a prize to the first finish who wasn't using Campagnolo equipment because it was such a rare thing.

WHILE A HUGE AMOUNT OF BIKES WERE SOLD DURING THE OIL CRISIS OF 1973 – US BIKE PRODUCTION WENT TO 15 MILLION IN 1973, UP FROM 4.7 MILLION THE PREVIOUS YEAR – THEY JUST WEREN'T USEFUL OR FUN TO RIDE – WHAT I CALL 'BIKE SHAPED OBJECTS'. ABSOLUTE JUNK HEAPS MADE FAST AND SOLD CHEAP TO SATISFY A SUDDEN RAMP UP IN DEMAND WHEN PEOPLE COULDN'T FILL THE GAS TANKS OF THEIR CARS. IT WAS A MASSIVE MISSED OPPORTUNITY THAT ALMOST CERTAINLY PUT MORE PEOPLE OFF CYCLING FOR GOOD THAN TURNED THEM ONTO IT.

Going off-road represented mechanical as well as mental freedom but finding the right bikes to work on wasn't easy. Nobody realizes this now but there were actually very few cruisers around in the 1970s.

Luckily I'd been working as a bike mechanic in shops since I was 14 years old, so I knew my way round a set of wrenches and I knew what would work. For example, I already knew that if a cruiser bike was pre-World War II the bottom bracket was higher for better ground clearance, essential on rough and rocky trails. They tended to be stronger and the geometry was better too. The big leap forwards was fitting proper gears so we could ride uphill and then proper brakes so we could race back down. That was the proper 'klunker' game changer.

Not everyone was into what we were doing. We used to have road bike club meetings at the Robson-Harrington community house in San Anselmo. One time somebody got their road bike ripped off from outside, so everyone used to bring their klunkers after that. Joe Breeze and Otis Guy used to give me such a hard time about my mongrelized bike when they rode over for the club meetings. They hated what we were doing and were telling me why it wouldn't work. Then we took them on an on off-road ride around the mountain and we totally left them. They were really strong accomplished riders who I had real respect for and we left them for dead.

Within two weeks they had gears on their klunkers too! Once more people got involved and there was an element of friendly competition as to who could pull off the neatest tech trick, that really spiced things up. We were always experimenting with things as a group too. Fred Wolf was this big dude who, like me, worked with Charlie sometimes. He was a real instigator of rides and the guy who came up with the name Repack, but he could snap pretty much any seat post. We even tried 7/8in steel posts from Schwinn exercise bikes because they were really thick and strong, but eventually we just ended up welding a triangulated post setup. You couldn't move it but you couldn't easily break it either and we started strengthening and modifying the frames with extra reinforcing tubes in the same way. We were still breaking them on a regular basis though, so pretty soon it was clear modifying existing bikes was always going to be really limiting.

That's when the first custom frames and forks started to appear and things really stepped up a level. Joe Breeze was first in our group with his 'Ballooner' frame with twin reinforcing tubes from head stock to rear axle but he took a while to build them so I had a frame made by Tom Ritchey. Tom was a young guy down in Redwood City, 50 miles away, but he was already making road frames and he made them really fast and really accurately. Scot Nicol (founder of Ibis Cycles), Tom Teesdale, Erik Koski, Terry Knight and a few others were all building frames too, but not one single person 'invented' off-road bikes. Don't get me wrong: I'm not trying to be revisionist here. There are all sorts of books, features and movies about those times and depending who's involved they all tell a slightly different story – just like this one does.

WE'RE ALL PART OF THOSE STORIES IN SOME WAY BUT WHAT WE DIDN'T DO WAS INVENT SOMETHING NEW

Sure, locally we were doing some things differently. But it was old news in a lot of places. 120 years ago everyone rode a bicycle off-road because there were no roads – everywhere was a dirt track. That didn't stop people riding, over mountains, through deserts, anywhere, or just fooling around for fun. There were guys in 1950s France – Vélo Cross Club Parisien – jumping in and out of bomb craters on bikes specially modified with suspension forks from mopeds and derailleur gears. They even used to race during breaks at motocross motorbike events. John Finley Scott had made his Schwinn-based 'woodsie' bike in 1953, then in the 1970s riders like Geoff Apps in the UK and Bob Crispin in Washington were building off-road bikes with gears, different brakes and bigger tires for their own personal amusement.

Kids all over the world were putting wider handlebars on their bikes, calling them trackers, scramblers, motos, whatever, and pretending they were motor-bikes. There were even some guys from Cupertino – the Morrow Dirt Club, they were called – who showed up to a cyclo-cross race in Marin in 1974 on geared cruiser bikes. Michael Hiltner – the 1965 US road race and hill climb champion, who renamed himself Victor Vincente of America after he set a double-transcontinental record in 1974 – started making small wheeled (20 and 24in) off-road bikes in Santa Monica. Around that time, while working at Wheels Unlimited bike shop in San Rafael, I built my first geared klunker. It took around a month to work everything out but it wasn't rocket science, it was just smart engineering.

These were all just solo projects or part of really small local scenes though. Tom Ritchey couldn't even sell the frames he made after mine because nobody he knew wanted them. A handful of frames and the market was totally swamped – that's how small the local scene was back then. What Charlie Kelly and I did was give this new type of bike a name. Then I took that product out of the village, personally spread it round the whole world and made an industry out of it, and that's the next big part of the story.

au cœur du sport

par Bernard DOLET

Américains et Soviétiques : même combat

Dans le Circuit de la Sarthe « open », qui a débuté vendredi, les coureurs amateurs américains et soviétiques seront plutôt alliés qu'en-nemis, pour faire face à leurs adversaires professionnels. C'est du moins ce que semble laisser entendre le geste conciliant de Gary Fischer à Sergei Morozov.

WHEELS, UNLIMITED

QUALITY BICYCLES SOLD & REPAIRED

1821 4th STREET - SAN RAFAEL, CAL.
PHONE 456-7279

97

Working as a tester at *Bicycling* magazine and being sent all the latest kit early was a real advantage. Because they knew I was into the kooky stuff not just the traditional they used to send me all the interesting gear.

That's how my first proper klunker came about in 1977. *Bicycling* sent me a Japanese Shimano Positron gear changer to test. It had push/pull cables and indexed indents on the derailleur itself so the gears would click into place. Everything else at that time was just done on feel and friction, which was fine on a smooth road but really didn't work over bumpy tracks. The Positron still needed cogs to work across though, so I modified an old Schwinn Excelsior frame to take an Exelu tandem hub. This was about the only hub that combined a hub brake and the threads for a freewheel, not just a single cog. Suddenly I could still pedal when other people were pushing on climbs and I could power down the hills too.

I hunted down some alloy rims that only weighed 19 ounces (540g) when other people were using 55-ounce (1,560g) steel rims. That really made a big difference. The bike was faster to accelerate and easier to handle too. The other big advantage was that the front brake still worked OK on alloy rims in the wet, which steel rims definitely didn't.

I can remember one time we were free form ridin out in this high pasture with really long grass and it had rained. Suddenly Wende Cragg – one of the original mountain bike riders and a really successf early racer – comes flying past me, totally out of control. The water on the grass was coating her st rims and the brakes just weren't working at all, so s had to just bail. She was lucky, man, because it wa just a field and so she just bounced and rolled an didn't hit anything, but that was a close call.

The front drum brake that came on a lot of Schwin bikes was terrible. It was this weedy little thing tha could barely slow down a bike on the flat, so it wa no use on a steep downhill. The cantilever rim bra that came on some other cruisers flexed so muc that they were even worse. That meant I took prop Mafac Tiger cantilever brakes which I used on my cyclo-cross race bike and teamed them up with th big German Magura motorbike brake levers. The added a lot more leverage than normal levers so brakes were really powerful, and if you've got goo brakes you can go a lot faster. Most of the other b I swapped around all the time to see what worked, but it was those Shimano indexed gears and Magu brakes that made the real difference. And both th brands would turn out to be a big influence on th evolution of the mountain bike.

onically the time I probably toned down my look the most was when I used to go to Repack. I was still racing
eriously on the road but I couldn't turn up in my road race kit. That would have looked totally out of place and
epack was a dangerous deal. We were regularly wrecking pretty hard and our clothes were the only protection
e had, so tough workwear was the way to go – thick denim jeans, Pendleton flannel shirts, Red Wing work boots
nd big leather rigger gloves.

MOST OF THE TIME BUILDING KLUNKERS WAS A SCAVENGER
UNT FOR RARE PIECES OF OLD KIT THAT WE COULD MODIFY.

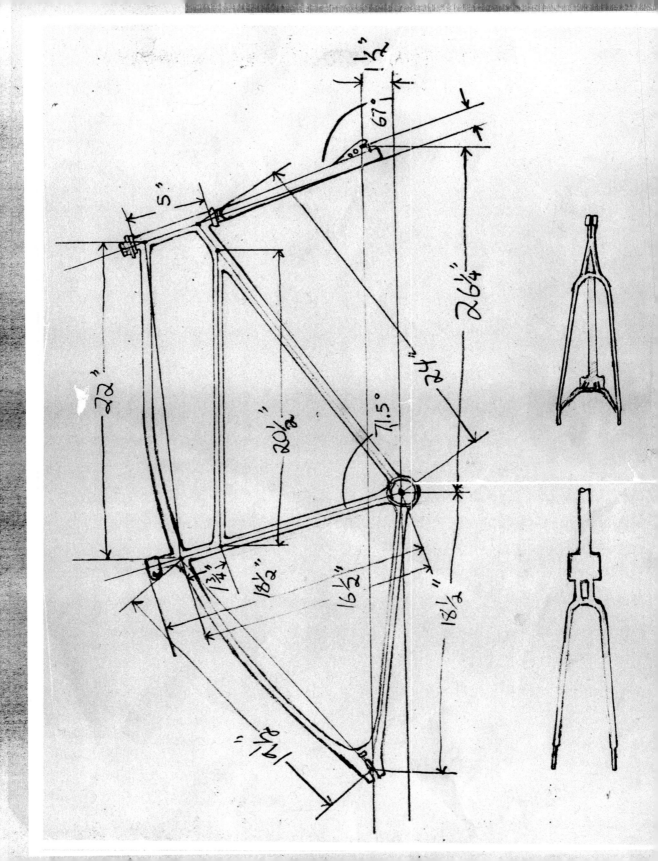

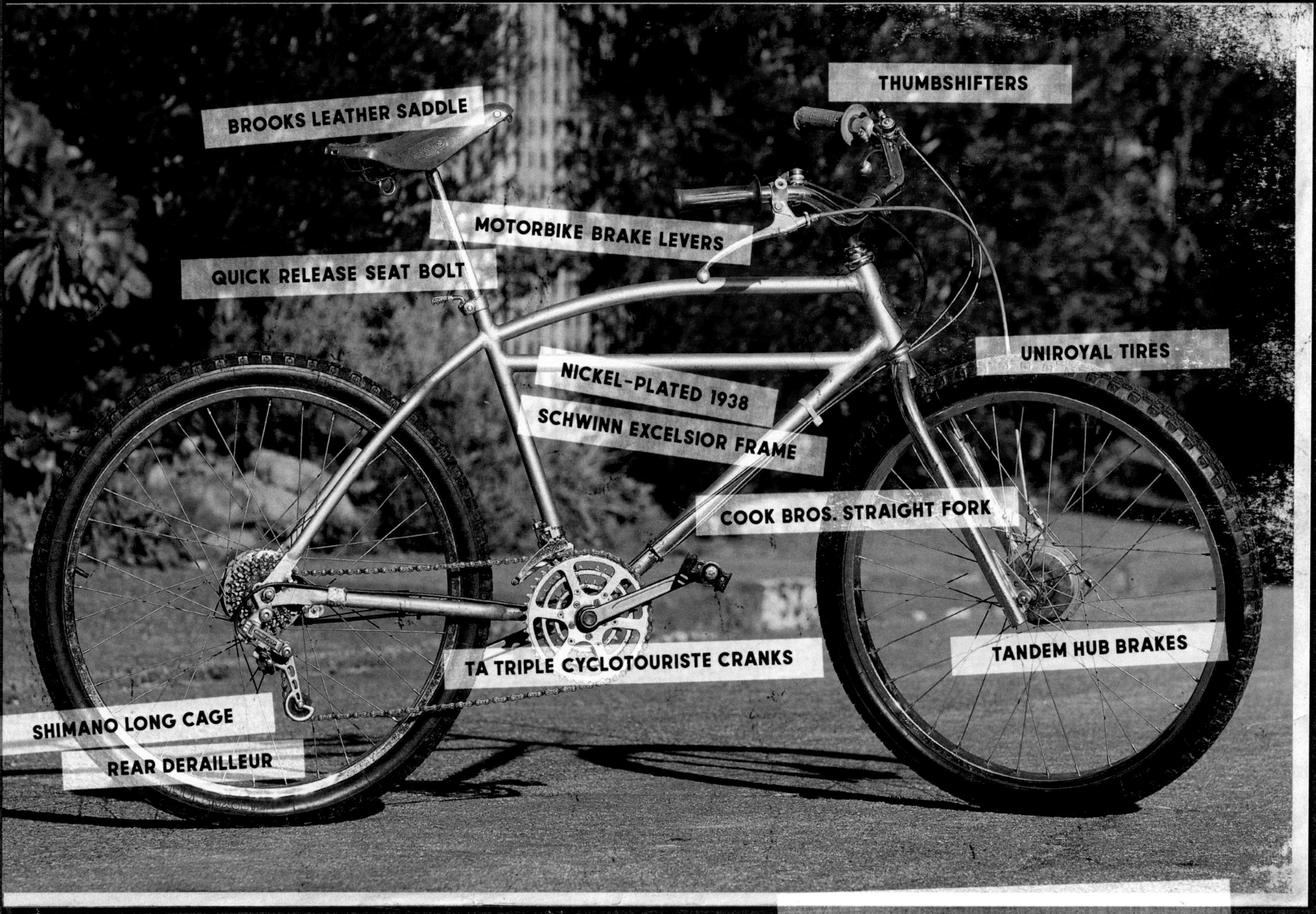

THUMBSHIFTERS

UNIROYAL TIRES

TANDEM HUB BRAKES

COOK BROS. STRAIGHT FORK

MOTORBIKE BRAKE LEVERS

NICKEL-PLATED 1938

SCHWINN EXCELSIOR FRAME

TA TRIPLE CYCLOTOURISTE CRANKS

BROOKS LEATHER SADDLE

QUICK RELEASE SEAT BOLT

SHIMANO LONG CAGE

REAR DERAILLEUR

The whole klunker story has been told so many times and everyone has their own opinions and timelines. What I do know is that I was the guy who made it possible for people to go into a shop and start mountain biking, so here's that story.

"October 1977, on top of Mount Barnabe, Marin County during the Moonset-Sunrise ride.
A map reading break with Joe Breeze and Eric Fletcher. I was on the 1938 Excelsior and Joe's on his Breezer Mk.1"

I'D ALREADY GOT MY KLUNKER PRETTY DIALED WITH THE DERAILLEUR GEARS AND THE MAGURA MOTORBIKE LEVERS WITH THE BIG CANTILEVE BRAKES. I WAS PRETTY HAPPY WITH THE SHAPE OF MY SCHWINN TOO, AS IT WAS AN OLDER ONE. I'D CHANGED THE FORKS TO COOK BROS CRUISER BMX FORKS THOUGH AS THEY WERE A LOT STRONGER. THEY ALSO HAD A 2IN OFFSET COMPARED TO THE ORIGINAL EXCELSIO FORK WHICH WAS 2.5 IN SO GAVE IT MORE STABLE HANDLING AT SPE

Speed was getting to be a big deal now because we had started racing on these bikes as well as just fooling around on them. It was always going to end that way because several of us were road racers anyway and you get any group of guys together and somebody is going to say 'hold my beer'. Repack was a totally different 'race' though. Not just because it was off-road on these crazy klunkers that we'd made but it was only two miles long and, after the first 50 yards, all downhill.

A lot of people think I was a big part of starting Repack but I wasn't. Fred Wolf was the main Larkspur ride organizer and he was the guy who got the key to the gate halfway down the course. He came up with the name Repack because you had to repack your coaster brakes with grease after each burning hot run or they just seized up. Charlie Kelly was the one with the timers and he did the admin and organizing. Charlie was really into it and he used to get so fired up we had to put a beer bottle top over the buttons to stop him from pressing them by mistake.

It was gnarly too. I'll be totally honest, I didn't enter the first one because I was chicken. I even took my cyclo-cross bike because I was scared I'd be talked into it if I turned up on my mountain bike. Instead I volunteered as one of the timers because I knew how setting off solo riders at regular intervals worked from time trials in road racing. I raced the second one though and after that I was gunning for the win every time.

"Go Team Plaid! Joe Breeze, Wende Cragg and Fred Wolf head up to the start of Repack at the top of Serpentine Hill on their Breezer Mk1s"

I realized pretty quick that Repack and racing mountain bikes were having an impact and a reach way beyond a few dudes fooling around for fun. People used to come up from town and watch the race. After I won people used to wander out of bars and tell me I had to "defend the name of Fairfax in that damn race". Nobody ever told me to do that with road racing.

A daily TV show called 'Evening Magazine' came out in January 1979 and did an eight-minute film segment about the Repack. It was proper coverage with us heading up the hill out of town in cattle trucks then drifting sideways through corners, crashing, whooping and hollering. They made it really look cool too, and that story went nationwide. There's a bit in that segment where I say: "It's come a long ways, and it's going to go a long ways." I realized mountain biking could really take off and I was already becoming the spokesman for it.

But it wasn't "going to go a long ways" unless we could make enough bikes for the people who were hearing about this race and seeing these programs. Sure some people were making frames but many they were slow. Some builders were making maybe 10 frames a year. Others were a bit faster but people could be waiting over a year for frames they'd ordered. And while some were beautifully made, with silver soldering and twin tubes, sanded down with 600 grit paper, and beautifully painted and plated a lot of them were breaking too because these guys weren't framebuilders or engineers. They'd put these beautiful, lightweight Columbus track fork legs into a solid crown with no external tangs or internal plugs and they'd just snap straight off. Others were made so tight that the silver solder couldn't ever get into the joints so there was nothing holding them together. If you crashed, the tubes would just fall straight out. At the other end of the scale, some of the other reinforced multi-tube bikes weighed even more than the original Schwinns.

Tom Ritchey had already made me a frame and he was really good. He was meticulous in how he prepared the tubes, so when he came to put the frames together he could do it really quick and they were really tight and accurate and needed very little finishing. He had another couple of guys doing the prep and finishing on them too, so it was a really slick, fast operation and he'd already made 100 road frames before he made the frame for me.

Once he'd made mine and one for himself, he made some more but he was based about 50 miles south of the scene and he just couldn't sell them. Anyway he rings me up and asks me if I can sell them for him and I think, sure, why not? I talk to Charlie and we turn out our pockets and we've got a couple of hundred bucks between us. We take that to the bank and open a checking account, and the name on that account I came up with was: MountainBikes. We were in business. I could have probably gone after other folks for using the name mountain bike after that, but I didn't. It didn't seem important at the time. Who knows what the whole industry would have been called if I had.

I grabbed some piano-moving blankets, jumped in this little beaten-up BMW I had, drove over to Tom, wrapped the spare frames up, and brought them back to this little garage we'd hired. Getting the frames was easy but actually making them into complete bikes, man, that was a challenge. You've got to remember nobody was making anything designed for what we wanted to do. We'd use pieces like the TA touring cranks from France because they had the right gearing but the arms would break after six months. The rings were really soft and they flexed all over the place if you pedaled hard. We also had to import Hurét's Duopar gears from Europe because they had this extra linkage that meant they were the only ones that worked with the wide range gears we used.

EVEN WHEN WE KNEW WHAT WORKED AND WHAT WE WANTED WE COULDN'T ALWAYS FIND IT. WE JUST HAD TO MAKE THE BEST BIKES WE COULD OUT OF WHAT WE COULD FIND, AND MOST OF THE TIME WE'D HAVE TO MODIFY MOST OF THE PIECES TO MAKE THEM WORK. I MEAN THAT WAS SLOW WORK AND IT WAS EXPENSIVE BECAUSE WE COULDN'T BUY ANYTHING IN BULK. WE WERE SENDING MANUFACTURERS OUR CATALOGS, BUT ONLY A FEW WERE INTERESTED.

Magura were the only company who extended us credit. They gave us $10,000 straight away which was pretty amazing as we were still just operating out of this garage, doing everything ourselves – I would buy the frame tubing, put it in my car and drive it down to Tom who would prep them and fillet braze them. Charlie and I would then go back, pick up the frames, take them to the painters, and then take them back to the MountainBikes shop. The only things we didn't do ourselves was anodize the components to make the custom colors. We did everything else: building, finishing and hauling the bikes, and we even hand printed our catalogs. We were doing the heavy lifting.

"Dennis 'Wiz' Leonard, building bikes in the San Anselmo workshop. He's since won awards in the film world for sound editing"

We had some pretty crazy moments. There was this one time when we had some bikes taken and somebody saw them being stripped down. So we went over straight away and me and Charlie just pile in and say: "Hey, those are our frames." We found out later the guy was a dealer and he'd just flushed a bunch of coke because he thought we were cops when we came busting in. So he was kind of relieved but also pretty pissed. We didn't care, we're used to the things getting crazy in the scene. Then we realize there's a bunch of parts missing so we get this guy to tell us where they are and it turns out that they're at this other dude's house. So we head over to this other guy's place and we go charging in at midnight and he jumps out of bed naked and comes at us and we're like "where's our damn parts?" and again he's like, "what?" So we turn the lights on and the parts are spread all around the room so we just grab his bedspread and pile everything in and run. It was gnarly man, but it was pretty funny too, just this guy stood there stark naked with no bedding wondering what the hell just happened.

Another time I'm unloading a box of tires in the street and this woman comes flying round the corner in her car and nearly kills me. I jump back so she just misses me but the car goes right over the box and it gets wedged underneath. So the box won't come out and I'm shouting, "my tires! my tires!" and I start raging at her. So she just hits the gas and goes tearing off with this big old cardboard box full of tires still wedged underneath her car. I run and grab my bike and I'm riding down the street as fast as I can, going "has anyone seen a car with a box of tires underneath it?" and people are like: "What? Who is this crazy dude?" So I get into the middle of town and I haven't been able to find her so I go to the police station to file a report for insurance. Anyway I'm in there describing what happened and this officer is thinking "what the hell" and then over his radio comes this call. "We got a car fire over here. It seems like there's something under the car, some rubber or something that's on fire, the car is totally engulfed in flames." So I jump on my bike and I ride over to where she is and her car is just this big ball of flames. I go up to her and I say "You gotta slow down, RIGHT!" That was kind of funny, plus she couldn't get away either – she certainly couldn't drive away – so I got her insurance details and we got the price of the tires out of her.

SO I JUMP ON MY BIKE AND
I RIDE OVER TO WHERE SHE IS
AND HER CAR IS JUST THIS
BIG BALL OF FLAMES.

Making the bikes was just a small part of it. You can make anything you want but mountain biking was onl
going to take off if people realized how much you could do on these bikes. Because of Repack people
thought they were only for downhill, so I set out to prove them wrong by racing them everywhere and ove
everything. Because that's what I do best, I put on a show! I started by riding the MTBs at cyclo-cross
races and I either came first, second or 10th depending on the course. Sacramento was sandy so the tires
floated and it went really well, but even on a course that didn't really suit the bike I was strong enough
to be up in the mix.

Being competitive on the bike was a real shock to people but the big breakthrough was winning the
Reseda to the Sea race. The idea of the race was that it would show which bike was the fastest from point
A to point B and the organizer, Victor Vincente, was sure it was gonna be his bike. He was a really good roa
rider and he had designed and built this 'mountain' bike called the Topanga. It was light because it used
small 20in BMX wheels so it accelerated real quick. But those little wheels didn't roll well, especially whe
the tracks were rough, unlike the 26in wheels we used. Anyway Victor was going to be there and some to
road racers and cyclo-cross riders were due to show up and I could see it was going to be a big deal so
we had to be there.

John Finley Scott, the guy who built that 'woodsie' bike back in '53, had this big double decker bus he'd
converted into the ultimate race vehicle. He'd taken all the seats off the bottom deck and put hooks in
the ceiling for hanging the bikes. There was a workshop downstairs too, while the upstairs had couches
and beds. It had this serious Perkins motor in as well, so that thing hauled. Anyway we showed up in th
amazing bus and everyone was like: what the hell? Then I pulled out my bike and everyone was even more
shocked. I mean you've got to remember that outside our Marin scene a lot of people had never seen a
mountain bike or even a klunker before. Traditional cyclists are exactly that – traditional. I even had someone
spit on my bike at a race in Pennsylvania just because they didn't like the way it looked.

BECAUSE THAT'S WHAT I DO BEST, I PUT ON A SHOW!

Anyway, I'm on the startline at the first Reseda and it was pretty much all cyclo-cross bikes apart from me. The race course was basically this really long paved climb and then a really long singletrack descent to the finish so I knew exactly what I had to do. I got a good start and then hung on in there all the way up the climb. Man they did everything to try and drop me, but they just couldn't. Like I said, I never used to get dropped on the road, plus long climbs suited me and I was determined to show what my bike could do. That chance came as soon as the trail pointed back downhill and got rough and from there I just dropped them like a stone. I mean they didn't stand a chance trying to keep up on cyclo-cross bikes with their skinny tires and narrow bars, and the small wheeled Topanga bikes really struggled and I smashed them too.

The people who were outraged by me and the bike managed to create even more publicity for my win because, as a United States Cycling Federation-registered rider, I shouldn't have been racing a quasi-illegal race like Reseda. That meant they made a big fuss about it in the *Southern California Cycling Newsletter* and the best thing was that they changed the name of the guy in second to protect him. Everyone knew who he was though as he was a top racer so that made my win even more remarkable. Because all the bike magazines were based in southern California it was a big deal for them too and we even got some mainstream press about it. Everyone wanted to know which was quicker off-road – cross bike, BMX or mountain bike – and I went right out and showed them.

PASSENGERS ARE NOT
PERMITTED TO RIDE
ON THE PLATFORM

"We brought a bunch of people down to the Reseda race in John Finley Scott's bus – with its big diesel engine – we were able to go 55mph up over the Grapevine out of Bakersfield, that hill is a real monster"

That first year I was one of the only riders on a 26in wheeled 'mountain bike', but by the next nearly everyone was riding them at Reseda and other races.

Even tiny events started to gain legendary status. The Pearl Pass challenge was just this low-key local thing that almost happened by accident. In 1975 some motorbike riders from Aspen in Colorado had ridden the old mining roads over the saddle of Pearl Pass to Crested Butte. Aspen was a high-end skiing town and these guys were flashing their money around in the Grubstake Saloon bar and generally being a pain in the ass. Fifteen of the Crested Butte guys who were proper hardcore mountain people – loggers and miners – decided to flip the joke on them next year and take their pedal bikes over the hill the other way. It's a brutal gig, only a few miles but really rough and the elevation tops out at 12,700ft so you're really struggling to breathe. They camped out half-way, several bikes seized up from overheating on the descent to Aspen, and only two riders actually rode the whole thing at the first attempt. The party they had at the Jerome Hotel and then around the rest of Aspen was a proper victory celebration though.

UP UNTIL THAT POI
BEEN DOWNHILL BIK
HIPPY SLACKERS I
MATTER WHAT I SA
FAST EVERYWHERE
ME . NOT ONLY HA
BIKES WERE FAST E
WE WERE PROPI
MOUNTAIN BIKIN

UNKERS HAD JUST
R A BUNCH OF
REPACK AND NO
BOUT THEM BEING
DY REALLY BELIEVED
ROVED THAT THE
OPLE REALIZED THAT
THLETES AND
OULD BE A
PROPER SPORT.

Anyways, we heard about it and in 1978 five of us headed over for the third Annual Pearl Pass Klunker Tour. I actually had to fly in from New York where I'd had a meeting for *Bicycling* magazine beforehand. The last leg of the journey was in a tiny four-seater Cessna prop plane. I had to take the front wheel off my bike and stick it across the back seats! The landing strip was just dirt, with rocks everywhere, so the pilot had to make a couple of circuits before coming in. All the time I could see the other guys from Marin just circling round at the end of the strip and this amazing mountainous landscape rising up all around. So we land, I get out the bike, put the wheel in, pull on my pack and I'm in heaven! Wende Cragg had come over as well and the locals were really surprised to see us there. That we had handmade frames, gears and brakes was a shock to them too, as they were still just on old singlespeed cruisers. They made us feel really welcome though and it was an awesome adventure that's become a proper annual event and race these days.

I've worked with pretty much every material, wood, stone, steel, aluminum carbon fiber, titanium, but sometimes the hardest material to work with is the grey matter between people's ears. That's just about marketing though and as the famous radio broadcaster Wes 'Scoop' Nisker said: "If you don't like the news, go out and make some of your own."

A lot of people seem to think publicity grows organically, or they want it to. That whole build it and they will come bullshit, but it just doesn't happen that way. Not quickly anyway. Even the guys who said I sold out acknowledge that mountain biking would never have taken off as fast or maybe at all without me. That's because the magazines didn't come to us, I went to them. I obviously had some good contacts from working at *Bicycling* so I just took the book that listed the circulation and ad revenues of all the magazines, wrote them down in order and started ringing the editors. My mom used to always tell me don't waste your time with the little guys, just concentrate on the big guys. She was a really successful realtor and businesswoman – which was rare back then – and she always told me to do a really good job of publicity and marketing. She helped promote my father's architecture business too and was great at getting them press coverage. She showed me the value of spending time getting the image, the tone and the story just right and crafting something editors could just put straight on the page. She would say: "You're doing their work for them so make sure it's at their quality or better or they'll just toss it out." We gave them all these little secrets so we became the go-to source of information for anyone interested in mountain biking.

123

We used our MountainBike brand name to create a huge storm of press exposure for the sport of mountain biking. We'd send press releases out to like 160 outlets all round the world and, in modern terms, we'd get millions of impressions. We even had a feature in *CoEvolution Quarterly* (the magazine of the Whole Earth Catalog) which was the first to talk about klunking and show the bikes. It had a sidebar on the Pearl Pass and Crested Butte races and everything. It was perfect non-endemic marketing. We just spread it around, got it hooked in everywhere, and watched the mountain biking waves ripple out all across the world. It was crazy.

That kind of smart guerrilla marketing works way better than just paying for conventional ads. Especially if you don't have any money! If I didn't have a contact I'd just cold call people on the staff and get in that way. Sometimes it took two or three times, which Charlie hated. I used to tell him to resubmit stuff that had been turned down as many times as it took. That's how we got into *Outside* magazine in March 1985 and ended up on the cover. It was a great shot too, with a female rider holding the bike over her head. She was the one who actually wrote the test piece as well, which opened up a whole other audience.

Charlie and I would go to the bike shows to meet people too. That human connection stuff is so important; it's hardwired into us. I saw a great example of that the other day when I took my little boy Robbie to a party. It was at 3pm. Normally he naps at 1pm but he's excited about the party and so he stays awake and then falls asleep on the way. When we arrive he wakes up and he is in a mess. He's tired, he's crying and he's inconsolable. The same thing has happened with his best buddy William, and he arrives in a real state too. Then they see each other across the party and, bang, suddenly they're smiling, running towards each other, laughing. They are just so happy to see each other, and that works on every level at every age. That was the difference between me and the other pioneers – I traveled and went and saw people and made those connections.

What's the best way to travel in remote areas? The Mountain Bike goes anywhere. Silently.

Balloon tires. 18 speeds. 28 lb.

Write or call:

Mountain Bikes

Box 405

Fairfax, CA 94930

(415) 456-1898

Those first couple of years were pretty crazy. We'd sold 160 bikes in the first year and then almost ,000 bikes in the second year. These weren't just any bikes either. We were doing some really cool stuff and conquering the high-end market. I was still working for *Bicycling* as a mechanic and road tester, and I'll always remember their salesman Bill Fields introducing me to Antonio Colombo at the Long Beach Bike Show. Antonio was a giant in the Italian and continental industry, the man behind Cinelli bikes and Columbus tubing. Bill said: "This is Gary Fisher, he makes and sells more $1,000 bikes than anyone else in the US!" That really made me sit up and realize what we'd achieved. Back then a top-end, fully Campagnolo-equipped Colnago race bike was $450. A full custom-built Ben Serotta was $995 and that was the best US-made bike you could buy. Our bikes cost from $999 to $1,300. My mother taught me that lesson from real estate – sometimes you need to raise the price to get the sale.

Some of the special custom orders were way more expensive too. We would charge up to $2,000 for our all black models. We had this really far out paint shop in San Marcos called Cycle Art that did these crazy tiger and zebra paint bikes. We even did a bike for Maxfields, a super high-end clothing shop in Beverly Hills. They needed it to really be something too, as they were off the scale. I mean they had Prada, but that was just tucked in the corner because it was the bread and butter stuff. So we made that bike as gold as we possibly could. Further down the line in the '80s we even did a build for the rock singer Sammy Hagar who had a string of shops. He was known as The Red Rocker because he loved wearing red, so we did a fully black build on a red frame – he bought two container loads.

It wasn't just the bikes we were pushing the limits with. We were doing a lot of other things in a totally different way from other bike companies. We had the only bike shop in the San Francisco Bay area – if not in the United States – where we wore suits and ties. I made it super-nice and clean. Even when we moved from the garage our showroom was still tiny. We would ask potential employees if they had ever worked on a submarine! But every fixture in there was carefully curated. It was like the Carousel ballroom all over again, a perfect little room filled with absolutely exquisite bikes. We achieved the look of someone very sophisticated from a very small space and our

WE SOLD HARD TOO. OUR FAVORITE LINE WAS :
" YOU DON'T WANT TO BUY A CHEAP PARACHUTE, DO YOU?"
PEOPLE WOULD COME OUT OF THE SHOP
LOOKING AT THE INVOICE THINKING
" WHAT HAVE I DONE!?!"

1

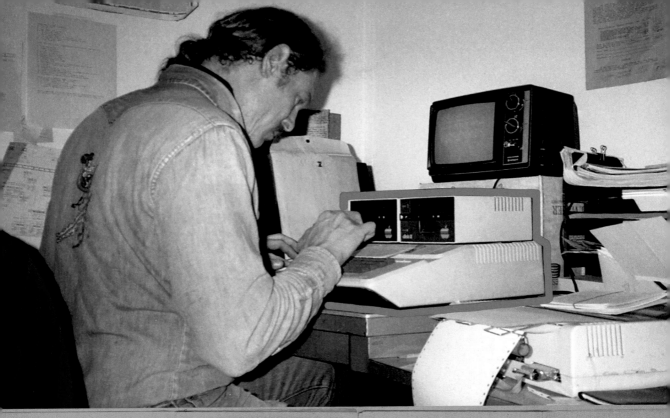

RITCHEY/MOUNTAINBIKE STANDARD SPECIFICATIONS

Frameset: Lugless brazed frame made with oversize chrome-moly and Reynolds double-butted tubing. Campagnolo seatpost quick-release, Campagnolo dropouts, Imron paint. Standard braze-ons include down tube water bottle cage bosses, cantilever brake bosses, derailleur and brake cable stops for split housing.

Bottom bracket: Sealed bearing Tom Ritchey custom.

Crankset: Extra-long TA Cyclotourist triple.

Pedals: BMX type with anodized alloy cage and chrome-moly shaft.

Rear derailleur: Huret Duopar "Eco".

Front derailleur: SunTour Compe V or VX.

Shift levers: SunTour Mighty Thumb shifter.

Handlebars: Tom Ritchey custom "Bullmoose" bar/stem.

Freewheel: Heavy-duty wide range 6-speed.

Seatpost: Extra-long SR Laprade.

Saddle: Avocet Touring II.

Headset: Chris King sealed bearing.

Hubs: Phil Wood 6-speed with allen-keyed end bolts.

Rims: Anodized alloy box construction 26 x 1.75 with polished braking flats.

Spokes: DT stainless steel.

Tires: Skinwall 26 x 2.125 balloon tires.

Brake Levers: Genuine Magura motorcycle levers.

Brake cables: Heavy-duty motorcycle brake cables.

Brakes: Mafac Tandem Cantilever.

Optional equipment and custom frame or parts work is available.

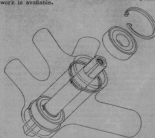

The _____ey sealed bearing bottom bracket is machin_____ the frame and is integral with the bottom bracket shell. This enables us to use larger bearings spaced further apart than in the Phil Wood BB. The Ritchey BB is also 36 grams lighter than the Phil at 251 g.

Dean Bradley

The MountainBike is also a fine city bike! Equipped with the new high-performance 26 x 2.125 skinwall tires, you will be nearly as fast as the ten-speed cyclist, with improved handling, braking, and resistance to the perils of inner city roads such as potholes, tracks, curbs, and sewer grates. Smooth riding and nimble handling make this a fine commuter bike, satisfactory in any weather conditions or traffic. The ruggedness we build in for use far from repair shops makes the MountainBike a dependable steed, with few of the tire and wheel damage problems associated with the more fragile lightweight ten-speeds.

For the BMX rider who is outgrowing his 20" bicycle, the MountainBike offers an alternative to motorcycles as an adult sport, and additionally fills the gap between BMX bikes and high quality road bikes.

The MountainBike satisfies the adult rider's desire for quality equipment while providing the ruggedness and stability of the 26 x 2.125 tire. High performance and ease of handling make this the ideal off-road or on-road all around vehicle

The MountainBike is the culmination of a six year program of research and development which began with the construction of the first multi-geared balloon tired bikes. These original hybrids proved to be the most efficient human powered form of transportation for off-road use and since then have been the subject of continuous improvement from the early "European/American crossbreeds" to today's highly refined machine.

Our back office operation was a real state-of-the-art set up too. We had 20 people sorting the components and putting the bikes together. We had seven different people building wheels. We had three different frame painters. We had a teletype machine for placing overseas orders and we were so on it we even got a computer in 1980 to manage the mail order database. Back then computers were super-primitive and it would still take four hours to sort 6,000 names by zip code, but it gave us a real edge on speed and selling and that was becoming more and more important as sales increased.

We knew other people were already making complete bikes and that bike shops were putting them together because they were buying components and build kits from us. Univega may have even had a complete mountain bike before us, and the Koski brothers at The Cove bike shop in Mill Valley definitely did. They teamed up with Mert Lawwill – he was a national championship-winning motorbike racer and engineer – and Terry Knight who was Mert's factory 'skunk works' welder at Harley Davidson and they made this beautiful BMX hybrid called the Pro Cruiser. It was full cro-mo steel frame with a small diameter, diagonal secondary top tube that really connected properly for extra front end strength. They had alloy rims that were pretty light, Cook Bros BMX forks, and thanks to Mert, they had totally radical 65-degree motorbike head angles for extra stability. People are only just getting switched onto that again 40 years later, but they made 500 of them before anyone else. Luckily for us they had flaws because of the sourcing. They only had a single chainring with nothing to hold the chain on and they had these itty bitty Sturmey-Archer street drum brakes with spiral wound cable housing. That gave them a really soft and spongey feeling, and if they got hot the pads were too small and they just didn't work. They were slow too because they had smaller wheels. I remember it took them three months to finish their catalog when we did ours in a week. Those guys and their designs were righteous though, and I worked with Mert Lawwill on our first full suspension bike a few years later.

Specialized were a growing parts importer who were already getting their Allez and Sequoia road bikes made in Japan. The owner, Mike Sinyard, was already riding a mountain bike he'd bought from me and getting his own version made in Japan was an obvious move. I suspected what might be about to happen though so the bike I'd sold him was kind of a reject. The forks were made by local builder John Padgett and they were too long, so the angles and ride height were out of whack. Sure enough when Mike did what I'd expected and the first Specialized Stumpjumper mountain bikes arrived from Japan they had that same incorrect geometry. Because there was no real standard, nobody even knew what was right or wrong. What did matter was that they were the same color as our bikes and selling for $750 – hundreds of dollars less than ours – and that really dented us. They were doing half page ads in magazines when we were still doing tiny corner adverts that you could barely fit a Haiku onto. One day someone rang up and asked if we did anything like a Stumpjumper. That really put us in our place.

Charlie was seething. In hindsight it was just a really good business move by Mike Sinyard. We'd had a great idea and were doing well. Why would he not try to do the same? Thankfully the first 125 Specialized mountain bikes sold out in a month, so we bounced back even higher because more people were hearing about this crazy new sport and getting into the whole scene. It gave us legitimacy too, because Specialized were already pretty well established in the US and Japan. Suddenly we weren't just this freaky brand doing our thing. We were part of a biking revolution and we were one of the originals too, which is always a strong position to sell from. But it was clear that if I was going to compete and keep my slice of the action, I needed to get my own complete bikes built out in Japan too.

Time is

"We used to ride our bikes real hard so we soon found out which components could take the hammer – like Campagnolo headsets"

Most of the first bikes we sold had a Ritchey frame (we had an A and a B model) and 'Bullmoose' bars which Tom also made for us, but the forks they came with varied. Tom used to make these amazing biplane crown forks but they took ages and he hated doing them, so he'd charge us $400 for each pair. That meant we used some other local builders like John Padgett or ready-made cruiser BMX forks from Cook Bros or even Tange and Ishiwata from Japan if we could get them. We used a mix of Japanese SunTour and French Hurét gears with a French TA crankset. We matched Mafac tandem brakes with Magura motorcycle levers and the rims were Ukai or Araya on Shimano and Bullseye hubs. We used a Campagnolo Nuovo Record cam lever to hold an SR seat post with an Avocet saddle.

Cyclists have always had this 'hot rod' custom upgrade mentality though, so we used to do some really neat specials as well. Our paint shop could do these awesome matt black or smoke finishes on components. We used to anodize TA chainsets gold and black and build wheels with super-light Ambrosio rims and Phil Wood or Dura Ace hubs. The Dura Ace hubs were great as they were the first with a free hub, which allowed wide spaced bearings. Otherwise the 185mm crank arms we used created so much leverage with the low gears that we used to destroy axles.

131

"Wende Cragg was one of the riders to get a bike from the first Ritchey batch and she was an incredible rider. This shot is from one of the Pearl Pass rides and she was always storming the pace"

We used Titanium Hurét derailleurs and stems that were silver solder welded into the forks below the threads. That meant we could remove the normal expander bolt and fit an exotic hardwood plug instead. These were made by Stevie Wilde, who used to make pipes and sculptures for the Grateful Dead. We even used to make our own custom brake cables with motorbike housing and our ferrules. We'd then offer custom paint on top of the component options.

We made some pretty neat stuff and one of the things I'm proudest of is that we raised the price people would pay for bikes. We made them luxury items that people would be really proud of. Making mountain bikes aspirational was a big part of our success.

"Sure, a few people were making similar bikes, but nobody was selling them as hard as we were with shots like these"

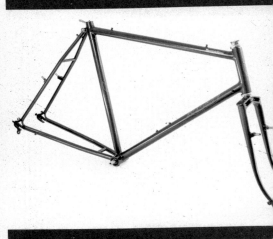

"The first Ritchey MountainBike frames were fundamentally cyclo-cross bikes with room for bigger tyres. They were beautifully made pieces that started a whole new sport

IF YOU DON'T MAKE NO EFFORT, YOU DON'T GET NO REWARD. THAT REALLY APPLIES TO HOW YOU DRESS.

...f you don't make no effort, you don't get no reward. That really applies to how you dress. It's just another way ...o market yourself and what you're selling. To be noticed as you enter a situation, whether that's at a meeting, ...conference or on TV. I have a reputation for looking kind of crazy and when I've got a point to make. The way I ...ee it is I want people to be looking at me, waiting for me to say something interesting and memorable – It's all ...part of the show.

PIONEERING IS A BITCH — MAKING SOMETHING NEW AND TRYING TO SELL IT IS REALLY HARD.

We'd had an incredible start with MountainBikes. Off the back of some friends having fun in the woods on modified vintage beach cruiser bikes we'd sold the media a whole new sport. Not only that, but we were successfully selling the most expensive bikes in the country as a result. Many of them to people who would never have thought of getting a bike before, let alone one costing over $1,000.

But trying to get frames and forks made and painted fast enough, scramble random components together from different suppliers at the right time and price, and then bolt it all together? Man, that was killing us. I knew the smart guys in the bike industry were wanting their own slice of the action, so it was obvious they'd be jumping on the bandwagon as soon as they could too. We'd left the other klunker builders a long way behind but now there was a real danger we'd be the ones getting dropped.

The answer was obvious, but it was a massive change and a big step up from where we were. What we needed was someone else to do all the hard work of creating complete bikes so all we had to do was open a container and sell them. The logical place to get that done was Japan.

Working with the Japanese was a total no-brainer. It was the start of the Japanese industrial invasion with cars and motorbikes from Honda, Nissan, Suzuki and others and the Japanese government already had offices in California to try and push their products and get more business. I had also road-tested a few bikes built in Japan through my work for *Bicycling* magazine and they were really good. Really well made and put together at excellent prices. Plus the Japanese were so keen to learn.

I MEAN WE WERE TINY AND TOTALLY IGNORED BY MOST PEOPLE IN THE US AND EUROPEAN BIKE WORLD, BUT THE JAPANESE WANTED TO SEE WHAT WE WERE DOING AND GET ON BOARD IN ANY WAY THEY COULD.

You have to remember that back then they had next to no market share at all, apart from really cheap equipment for throwaway bikes. I can remember talking to Yozo Shimano, the head of what is now the biggest bike component manufacturer in the world. He was wondering out loud if they would ever have components on a bike that would win the Tour de France. That was an almost impossible dream for him in the early 1980s. Since 1999 they've won 17 yellow jerseys and it's rare that any bike in the Tour doesn't have a complete Shimano groupset.

ut this was nearly 40 years ago and they were desperate to find the next step up into the market after BMX. They really got the whole nature side of things too; that our bikes were a great way of going out and exploring the wilderness. Shimano were primarily a fishing brand so they really understood that whole meditative, health boosting side of being outdoors.

It wasn't just Shimano interested in working with us, either. Right from the start we had hundreds of different visitors from Japanese industry and trading houses come to see us, to talk to us about what we were doing and how they could help. In that time we'd only had a handful of visits from European representatives and the only US brand who came to see us was Schwinn. They were still massive at the time and the last big industrial bike power in America. Even though they made the Excelsior beach cruisers that our first bikes were based on, they just didn't get it. They made their own bike that they thought looked right but it was a total mess. They called it the Klunker 5 even though nobody was calling mountain bikes klunkers anymore. It had this weedy little caliper brake on the front and a drum brake rather than a coaster brake on the back, so it could barely stop on the flat let alone on a proper descent. It had steel rims that weighed a ton and a bottom bracket that was too low for pedaling. The frame tubing was cheap so it was super-heavy and, while it kind of looked like it should work, in reality it was absolutely no good for riding off-road. Like many of the established brands, they just didn't care. They were just about the look and making a quick buck.

The only US guys who really got it were the BMX dudes like Cook Brothers. Many were local and they could see the similarities between how things were happening for us from back when BMX was starting to grow. The BMX boom had passed though and so they needed something new. Mountain bikes were the obvious up-and-coming craze so they were on it straight away, modifying 24in wheel Cruiser BMX forks for bigger 26in wheels and also making us brand new components to replace the stuff we broke.

Interest from Japan really took off after Charlie and I did a presentation for *Bicycling* magazine at the New York bike show in 1981. Like always we'd really done our homework – we'd been rehearsing the presentation for over a year beforehand. We actually got to use George Lucas's private screening room in Hollywood to practice because Howie Hammerman, one of the original klunker crew, was George's third employee at Lucasfilm.

HOWIE WAS THE SOUND ENGINEER THERE AND ACTUALLY ENDED UP BEING JABBA THE HUTT'S BELCH IN 'RETURN OF THE JEDI'.

Anyway our presentation was tight, with some great pictures of Wende Cragg riding our bikes taken by her then-husband Larry Cragg, and we sold the whole idea of MountainBikes really hard. Right after that presentation we were approached by Jimmy and Chen from the Far East Trading Company. Their main business was importing pearls but they were wanting to diversify and realized that bikes could be the next big thing. So they saw the presentation and they were like: "You REALLY need to come to Japan" and so they lined up a trip full of meetings and factory visits for us.

I know some people struggled to adapt to the food and other aspects when they first went to Japan but for me it was no big deal. In fact I couldn't wait to get over there and see what it was like for real as I'd heard so many stories from my Japanese aunt and my Japanese best friend from back when I was a little kid. I was used to the culture and cuisine because of both them and their families. Western food out there is always a bitter let down and amateur Japanese food can get pretty challenging sometimes, but Japanese professional food is amazing. I can eat that all day.

The hippy movement philosophy was based on east meeting west too. The whole idea of Zen, being reserved, respectful, polite and appreciating the moment had a lot of parallels to the counterculture.

JUST LITTLE STUFF LIKE NOT TEARING INTO A MEAL STRAIGHT AWAY I MEAN IF YOU TRY AND POUR YOUR OWN DRINK IN JAPAN, MAN, IT'S JUST NOT GOING TO HAPPEN. THE CULTURE IS THAT YOU ALWAYS TAKE CARE OF THE OTHER PERSON YOU'RE WITH FIRST BECAUSE YOU'RE HAVING YOUR EXPERIENCE TOGETHER.

I've always really liked that approach. It feels natural. I loved it and I still do.

One of the best compliments I ever got was from Nota San from the Kozaki Trading Company, who we did a lot of business with. He once told me:

"YOU'RE MORE JAPANESE THAN SOME JAPANESE!"

I was really proud of that. I can still sit on my haunches now because of meetings with distributors, dealers and mechanics in south east Asia, where we all sit low down to talk in meetings or work on bikes. Why should you expect people to change the way they naturally behave just so it's comfortable for you? If you make the effort the other way that's not just respectful, it creates a really positive connection.

Anyway I knew that this was going to be a serious business trip so I had to look right. I went into Wilkes Bashford, the most famous couture store in San Francisco, and bought this amazing Ralph Lauren suit. By this time I was already used to people thinking I was totally selling out because they told me to my face. They'd been doing that since we started making a business out of 'their' hobby. When we started wearing suits in our little shop some people really got upset. In a way I guess I was selling out, but I saw it as selling something awesome, something that shouldn't be kept secret. I wasn't ashamed of doing that at all, I was proud of it.

ALSO PEOPLE HAVE THIS IDEA OF WHAT HIPPIES LOOKED LIKE AND HOW THEY BEHAVED – BASICALLY GETTING STONED AND DOING NOTHING – BUT THE ORIGINAL HIPPY IDEA WAS NOTHING LIKE THAT . IT WAS ABOUT EXPANDING YOUR MIND SO YOU COULD DO MORE, BE MORE CREATIVE, FREE YOURSELF FROM LIMITS.

The way we saw it, it was about celebrating yourself and being happy with what you are, and part of that is dressing well and projecting your character. I was selling this amazing thing we had to the rest of the world, and that meant we needed bank loans and we needed the support of serious Japanese business. As honest as Charlie was, he looked like a hippy and nobody was ever going to lend us serious money if we both looked like that. Anyway it obviously worked because even the Japanese government came on board and gave us an $80,000 loan.

While the food and culture wasn't a shock and I was suited and booted for serious business, I couldn't believe just how frantic Japan was. Right from when I stepped off the plane, just how busy and how fast-paced business was, it totally blew me away. I remember arriving in Tokyo station and thinking: "I have never seen this many people in my entire life. Literally the number of people I can see right now is equal to all the people I have ever seen!" It was crazy. Businessmen were literally running through streets and sprinting between trains to make their next appointment. They were right on it, turning it over, straight onto the next meeting, then the next. I'd never seen anything that aggressive or fast-paced. It was such a culture shock. People worked really hard! Back then if you acted like that in the US people would think you were crazy.

I was really struck with how precise things were too. We took the bullet train to Osaka, Kobe and then Sakai city and sometimes you only had three minutes to make connections because everything was so on time. They were trying to hustle all the time and you had to hustle too to make some of these connections. It paid off to be fast!

It was pretty full on, but I wanted it that way. This was a project that I really needed to work. I wanted to find a bike builder. I wanted to get not only get frames or complete bikes but also parts. I wanted to have everything I needed to make a bike in one box.

I went to Japan seven times in 1981 and I saw some totally amazing things on each trip. Junzo Kawai who was head of SunTour – then a massive Japanese component powerhouse – arranged a meeting for us at the Panasonic bike factory. It was totally unlike anything I'd ever seen. Everything was automated. Cutting, mitering, jigging, everything. The tube joints were even pre-filled with brass rings ready to mel and form the connection when the brazing robots got to work. The tubes would literally go in at one end of the process and the frame would come out the other end without being touched by a human hand Think about that. Nobody touched the frames at Panasonic apart from the decal application and nobody was doing anything like that with bike manufacture – it was rare in any industry back then.

Another company, Ishigaki, were going to do these immaculately TIG welded frames for us. TIG welding awesome because it's a cleaner, lighter construction method. It's how nearly every mass-produced ste frame is made now but at that time you just didn't see TIG welded bikes being made in the US, apart fr by a few specialists like Mert Lawwill and Terry Knight. Everything back home was either fillet brazed b hand – which took forever unless you were very skilled – or used tubes plugged into sockets (lugs) at th frame junctions. In Japan I was seeing the future of framebuilding right in front of me and it was so excitir

Mounta

Much more than a cruiser, the MountainBike is the most expensive balloon-tire bicycle on the market. Built for high performance on any terrain, MountainBikes are consistent winners in off-road races with victories this year at Reseda

Send 25¢
for information:

MountainBikes
P.O. Box 405
Fairfax, CA 94930
(415) 456-1898

nBikes

(13 miles), Lopez Lake (25 miles), and Sespe Hot Springs (36 miles).

A hand-brazed Chromoly-Chrome-manganese frame, 3 x 6 gears, and 27 lb. total weight make this the most versatile bicycle you can own. See us for custom off-road bicycles and supplies.

We also toured a lot of the component suppliers, but you rarely dealt with them individually. In Japan every thing was controlled through different trading houses – effectively brokers between you and the individu brands. The Kozaki Trading Company handled SunTour, Sugino and Dia Compe. Shimano used the Rio Maru trading house but we also visited Shimano themselves and again it blew us away. We saw such incredibl machinery. There's a famous room where you go in and it's totally dark but there's just this deafening nois of metalworking. Then they switch on the lights and it's just this whole army of different robots making component pieces and assembling gear derailleurs with not a single person in there. Compared to our operation – or anything I'd seen before – it was like science fiction! Shimano were working on aerodynam road components at the time too and they'd built their own wind tunnel in the factory to test them. It wa so far ahead of anything I'd seen or even heard of elsewhere.

As well as being really open to new ideas, the Japanese were really straight to do business with. Most countries you can play one vendor off against another to get the best price. The Japanese will all just ring each other and come back with the same price, so there are no wild deals. I'm sure they made a really good profit on our bikes but so did we and we sold every one we could get, so everyone was super-happy.

WAS SO EXCITED TO BE
ORKING WITH THESE GUYS
ND THEY WERE SO EXCITED
O BE WORKING WITH US TOO.
HEN IT CAME OUT, THE
HIMANO XT WAS THE FIRST
PURPOSE-BUILT MTB
ROUPSET WHERE EVERYTHING
AS DESIGNED TO WORK
OGETHER PERFECTLY. AND
INCE IT LOOKED LIKE A SET
F SYNCED PIECES RATHER
HAN A JUMBLE OF JUNK, IT
ADE A MASSIVE DIFFERENCE
O HOW OUR BIKES LOOKED.

e I said, I was so excited about the potential of
at they could produce for us, but not everyone
e was happy.

Unfortunately my relationship with Tom Ritchey began to fall apart right from the first trip to Japan. Tom was an awesome framebuilder and together I thought we could rule the world. But during that trip he first got ill and then it became very clear that he didn't want the same things I did. I wanted to get good quality, affordable frames built into complete bikes. All he wanted to find was a new set of lugs so he could build cheaper lugged frames as well as the fillet brazed ones, and then we could carry on building complete bikes. Things were tense on the trip.

When we got back I was planning to send drawings to Japan to get the frames produced. Tom said it would be better if he sent a frame for them to copy instead and I thought: "Yeah, OK, maybe that is easier." Three weeks later the frame comes back but the geometry is wrong. I'm like "what the F?" so I go straight down to Chinatown to buy plane tickets – you could get them faster and cheaper that way – and two days later I'm in Japan laying their frame on top of the one that Tom sent over and they're exactly the same. He was trying to frame the Japanese builders. It was a very delicate situation as I was still buying a lot of frames from Tom and I still wanted to, but things went south very quickly after that.

Charlie was unhappy too. He'd never really been comfortable as a salesman and he wasn't interested in the business side of things. And business wasn't great at that point. We had $80,000 of debt, now Tom was selling against us, and we were having issues with suppliers because of rumors we were going bust. It was really tough and Charlie was done with it. He just wanted to sit in the back and build wheels and I didn't blame him. In the end we just went for a walk round the block to talk it out and I gave him a bike, a computer and forgiveness of his half of the debt. He was proper pissed, it was a proper divorce. We dissolved Mountain-Bikes and I set up Gary Fisher Mountain Bikes in its place.

I always knew writing this book would be partly writing a business lesson.
It seems like at one time or another everything that could happen did happen.
Sometimes it was great and sometimes it was unbelievably, truthfully bad.
This was definitely one of the worst of times.

Thankfully all the bikes I'd had made in Japan arrived later that year. They totally
turned things around. Two 40-foot containers full of ready-made bikes that were
pre-sold before they even got to us, so they went out as fast as we could unload
them and address them. We were selling them mail order, retail and wholesale.
All over the US, then Canada, then the UK, then all over the world. Boom! It was
beautiful. By the end of 1983 Tom, Charlie and I were done but I'd turned that
$80,000 debt around and I'd made $100,000 on top.

Everything came complete too. We were used to scraping stuff together to try
and make complete bikes in the US but over there they had it all to hand, all ordered
to be there exactly when they needed it. They wouldn't even ship a bike if
there was a part missing so all we had to do was get them out of the container,
check them over and then collect the checks from customers who couldn't
get enough of them.

The Japanese loved having us in their factories because they could show the other competitors what w
were going to do the next year. Fisher was still a tiny little company compared to other established bike
brands but we were certainly the innovators and developers. I soon started using wider hubs as it mea
the spokes were further apart. The more we triangulated it, the stiffer and stronger it was, and when
we went from 125mm to 135mm all the wheels that had been collapsing started lasting. Shimano start
making that available to everyone but I was the guy that pushed them to do it. I was like: "Come on, this
way too easy to do, this is just a win all the way!"

It also meant we could use really radical equipment like Shimano Dura-Ace road racing hubs. They had th
latest free hub technology rather than freewheels which meant the axles were better supported and
stronger too. We also used long arm Shimano road gears, because they were lighter and more accurate
than the touring gears, and that was a big part of developing the XT groupset.

We were experimenting with geometry too, because up to that point the numbers were pretty similar to road bikes just with fatter tires. I remember some Canadian guys saying that to us in the early days and Charlie getting really offended. But they were right. The 1987 Procaliber was the first bike where we slackened off the head angle a little and it was called the best-handling off-road race bike ever, so soon everyone was using our numbers. I even built some forks up using Campagnolo rear track dropouts (the wheel holding pieces) so we could slide the wheel back and forward to change the offset of the fork and how the bike handled. I asked Paul Turner to build me some forks like that. He was a motorbike mechanic and suspension specialist who was starting to work with mountain bikes too and already developing the first RockShox suspension fork with Keith Bontrager (another motorcross engineer turned mountain biker, who ended up selling his company to Trek too). Those first RockShox forks used a bolted crown so instead he sent me several different fork crowns to try. After about three months switching around we ended up with 38.1mm (1.5in) and that became the standard for the next 40 years. It was all about evolving the mountain bike into something that was properly worked out rather than just being this haphazard mash-up of kit and angles. I still love to get involved with stuff like that now when I can.

By the late '80s I was introducing even more radical ideas to the mass market. I teamed up with Richard Cunningham to make a mass production version of his Mantis XCR. It was a totally radical design that meant we could use large diameter aluminum alloy tubing for the front end, but still keep steel for the back end. We couldn't use an alloy back end because the technology for bending and shaping aluminum tubes like that just didn't exist back then. We couldn't weld steel onto alloy either though so instead we bolted the back end on. We called it the CR7 and people loved those bikes, reviewers, riders everyone. I posted some pictures of it on Facebook a few years back and people were still raving about how much they loved their CR7s. Some were still riding them 35 years later.

We introduced a totally new oversized head bearing standard on that bike too. By that point I was already using a really early computer program to develop my tubing. It told me what type of wall thickness, what type of modulus of elasticity, weight and so on I'd get out of different dimensions and tubesets. It was clear we couldn't use a small inch tube as it didn't give a big enough joining surface onto the big alloy frame tubes, so I put in the numbers for an inch and a quarter headtube. By doing that we made the frame stronger and we stiffened up the fork and the stem about double too. We called it Fisher Evolution Oversize.

In the early days, I used to take a road bike and a mountain bike to Japan so I didn't miss out on my miles. I'd been going really well on the bike. I was actually on the Olympic team long list for the road race until the US decided to boycott the 1980 games in Moscow. Domestically I was fast and I raced well but everyone would just chase my little ass down, nobody wanted me to win. I was a marked man from the first criterium we did that year, where I escaped with half a lap to go and only just got chased back by two riders. After that they never let me get away again. I could always be a domestique, supporting other riders, but being the leader wasn't going to happen, so I soon pretty much gave up on being serious on the road.

I did a bit of mountain bike racing out in Japan. They had a downhill race which they tried to make like Repack which was pretty crazy. It was super sketchy and most of the riders had no idea what they were doing, but the enthusiasm was awesome and it was amazing to see the sport spreading round the world.

That made mountain bike racing the obvious choice both for me to have fun and to spread the Gary Fisher Mountain Bikes name further. There was some really good, well-organized racing starting to happen outside California. They even bought European riders over for some events.

We created a really good Fisher Mountain Bikes team too. We set the first team up for the Santa Rosa Rock Hopper Race in 1982. We had custom bikes and team jerseys just like a pro road team. We also had a ringer on the team. Eric Heiden was a world record breaking speed skater who won every short and long course skating event at the 1980 Olympics. Nobody had ever done that before – or has since. He then turned pro on the road for 7-Eleven but on a mountain bike he wore a Fisher jersey. I knew Dale Stetina from road racing too – he was a two-time national champion and he won the Coors Classic Stage Race twice but he raced for us at the Nationals in '83.

Our more regular riders were amazing too though. Jacquie Phelan was an awesome rider physically and she was one of the first female mountain bike icons. She had no tactics – she'd lead out from the middle of the road in a crosswind but she was a real classy, strong rider and a real fighter. At the first Whiskeytown DH in Colorado, I won the race by 15 minutes but Jacquie got 12th overall, winning the women's race by miles and beating most of the men too.

Wende Cragg was a superb rider from the early days of Repack right through to the first international downhill World Cups over a decade later. She was the first woman to ride the Pearl Pass rides out of Crested Butte and always won prizes at the klunkers banquet for her race wins. I know she got the perfect attendance prize for sure. And the photography she and her then-husband Larry Cragg did for us was probably even more important than her results for growing the brand.

Mike Kloser and Sarah Ballantyne were great athletes and, crucially, did great interviews too. So when I found out that this crazy dog sled and skier race across Alaska in like minus 40 temperatures was being opened up to bikes, I thought: "This is an ideal match, these guys are from Colorado, they live in the mountains, they can handle any conditions." So off they went to Alaska to complete in Iditabike – and it worked. They both won and that created amazing publicity way beyond normal mountain bike racing. Racing a bike through the snow and ice at 40 degrees below was clearly an insane thing to do, so even regular people in the street wanted to read about it. Jimmy Deaton was another guy who did great things on our bikes. He won a bunch of races for us, including the Kamikaze downhill race at Mammoth Mountain in 1985 and '88 (and '92, '93 and '94, but that was on a Yeti).

Joe Murray was the first true Fisher Mountain Bikes racing star though. He started working for us as a floor sweeper but he was soon the fastest bike assembler we ever had. He could build 14 bikes in one day, and he was just as quick at racing. As soon as he started competing he won. He went to Colorado for the Nationals, lost the first two races then took a week off to get used to the altitude and came back and beat Andy Hampsten. I mean Andy was a real legend, he was the first American to be really competitive in Europe in the biggest classic and stage races and he won the Giro d'Italia in 1988, but Joe had the better of him.

We created a huge amount of attention around thes[e] races and our successes, even though sometime[s] there'd only be maybe 100 people there including people's dogs or hikers who just be happened to b[e] walking past. Nobody looked too hard at that thoug[h] because we gave them great stories and great pictures to go with them, exactly like how my mom had taught me. *Winning* magazine would just use our press releases verbatim and they even put Joe in their 1985 poster line up alongside legendary Tour de France winners Bernard Hinault and Greg LeMond. That was a massive deal as it showed mountain bikes and mountain bike racing were now really on the cycling map.

It wasn't just the specialist media either. We got racin[g] stories and Joe Murray features into publications like *MAD* magazine as well as big lifestyle magazines lik[e] *Vanity Fair.* We got a Joe story into an army magazin[e] called 'On Your Own' that had an 11 million circulatio[n] among high school kids. We had a full-page photo in the German lifestyle magazine *Bild*. So our bike[s] and our riders were appearing all over the world, and where those stories went, the sales followed.

Racing was great for product development as well as for marketing. When you're flat out, giving it everything, that's the ultimate testing crucible where only the best components and ideas survive. Joe Murray was really into helping us with development stuff and he was also a secret 'skunk' development rider for Shimano. They were so into it that we even had the legendary Shinpei Okajima – the head ideas man from Shimano – working and racing with us for three months. He was an accomplished track and road racer but MTB was all new. He took a tremendous spill in the first race and I felt so bad as he was laid up for weeks but he stuck at it. He developed SIS (Shimano Integrated Shifting) click stop gearing for mountain bikes and he and Joe played around with all sorts of cable arrangements, cable guide positions and alignments. While with us, Shinpei also did a lot of the groundwork for Shimano Deore XT. The introduction of the first ever dedicated mountain bike groupset was a massive deal and meant Shimano had the performance off-road market wrapped up overnight.

Racing and publicity don't always go your way though. Just when it looked like Joe Murray was unstoppable – in 1984 he won eight events in a row and followed it up the next year with 12 straight wins in the US national MTB series NORBA, a record that's still unbeaten – things went sideways big time. It was mostly to do with relationships and other stuff, some of it really heavy, that I didn't know about at the time because we'd had a real communication breakdown. The result was that he just wasn't interested in putting in the big training miles anymore. The team's riders weren't doing the races I wanted them to either and they were getting beaten up by our arch rivals in the Ross Indians team. Because I didn't know any of the back story to Joe's unhappiness I was seriously pissed off, so when I got approached by Bob Buckley from Marin Bikes wanting to sign him I was happy to sell him his contract. I also sold Bob the name 'Marin Mountain Bikes'. He was already using it because he didn't realize I'd registered it for a fillet brazing factory. I ended up using Tom Teesdale to do my premium framebuilding instead so I didn't need the name. Bob was a good guy though, always easy to deal with and be around so I just said, "I'll sell you the name for $1,000" and it was cool. Not everything has to be as difficult as some people seem to want it to be!

Anyways Joe does one of his first races for Bob with his bike painted up in the colors of this new brand Marin but the bike breaks and he's raging about it. Then he scratches the paint off and shows people it's his old Fisher frame. Thing is it was the bike we'd used for the Shimano cabling experiments and it broke exactly where we'd done all these different braze ons! That part of the frame had seen so much heat the steel was just ruined, it would have had no strength at all. But the damage to our reputation was already done.

EVEN BACK THEN WITHOUT THE INTERNET THAT KIND OF BAD NEWS TRAVELED FAST AND IT CAN BE REALLY HARMFUL.

The Japanese side of things was changing as rapidly as the racing side. In 1982 when we got the first delivery of complete bikes we were getting 250 yen to the dollar. Within a few years it was down to 100 to the dollar and that meant our costs were going through the roof. We hung on for as long as we could, but soon it became clear the Japanese adventure was over. Taiwan was now the only direction to go. That was a totally different society and a different way of doing business, one that I wasn't used to. It was a whole new chapter for me and Fisher bikes.

"A top ad executive who was a customer of ours came up with the "Best Engineered All-Terrain Vehicle For Under $35,000." We were having to fight back hard against newcomers like Specialized and Univega so we really tried to leverage our experience and quality. And cool paintwork"

"The first Japanese bikes to come through were actually badged as Montare MountainBikes not Fisher MountainBikes. At only $610 and just about ready to roll straight from the container they were total game changers for us."

HE COST OF QUALITY

...kes under the chainstays, bolting the Bullmoose bars ...aight onto the forks, using Hite Rites on the seatpost and ...-round Biopace rings on the chain sets. If we thought it ...uld give us an edge, we were into it"

...ur buddy Joe Breeze helped design the Hite Rite as the first ...opper seat post and we stuck with the design for a while"

...n a team bike like this one, Fisher Team racer Jimmy Deaton ...as the first 'Kamikaze' downhill winner at Mammoth ...ountain in 1985

While by the early '80s I knew that Japanese-made bikes were the only way to be competitive and keep up with the market we were creating, I was worried that having bikes made in Japan rather than US would be a problem for some people. We never had any issue though. The bikes were really well made, really pretty, and they were from us, so people trusted in our reputation for quality. We called the Japanese-built bike the Montare. It was so well made that the fillet brazing never needed cleaning up, so the factory saved a load of time and money that way. Not every one was perfect close up, so we dropped the gloss black and gloss white paint options because they would highlight any blemish. Instead we used a metal flake finish that was perfect for hiding any irregularities, and once they saw the prices people just didn't care where they were made. We had a US-built bike called the Mt. Tam – after the mountain we used to race Repack on – which was basically exactly the same as the Japanese-made Montare but cost an extra $350. Soon as the Montare arrived, nobody bought it.

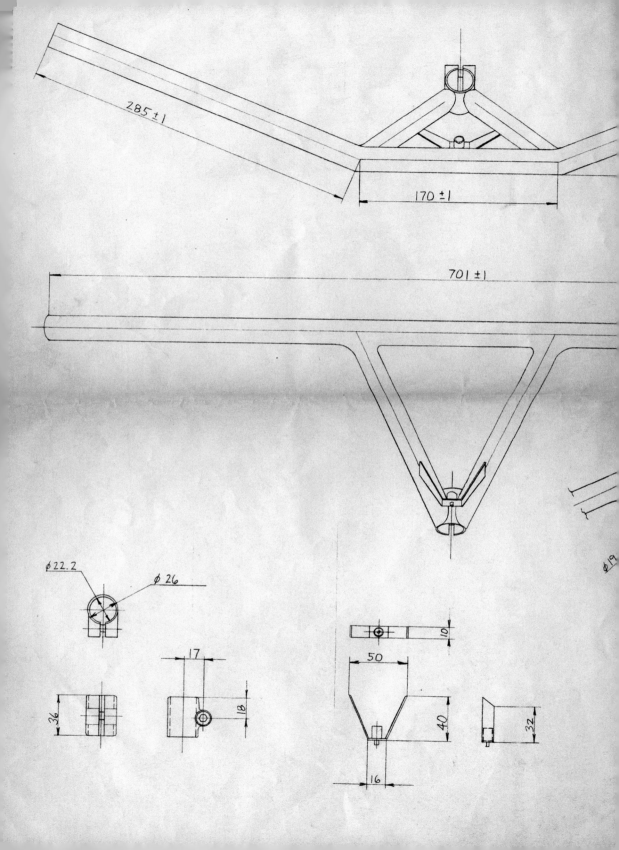

285 ±1

170 ±1

701 ±1

φ22.2

φ26

φ19

17

18

36

50

10

40

16

32

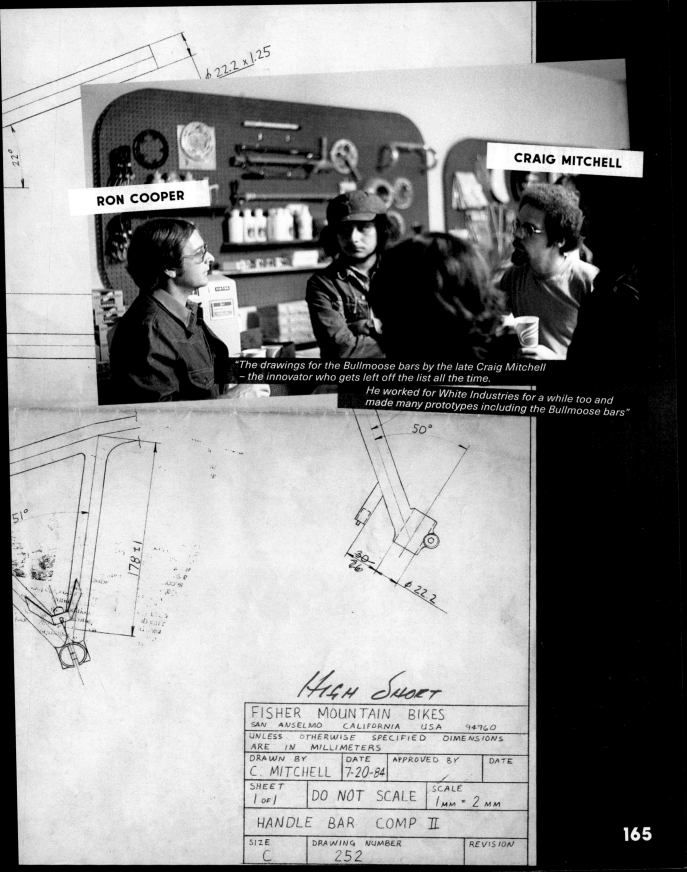

ø 22.2 x 1.25

22°

RON COOPER

CRAIG MITCHELL

"The drawings for the Bullmoose bars by the late Craig Mitchell
– the innovator who gets left off the list all the time.

He worked for White Industries for a while too and
made many prototypes including the Bullmoose bars"

50°

51°

178 ±1

30
66

ø 22.2

High Short

FISHER MOUNTAIN BIKES			
SAN ANSELMO CALIFORNIA USA 94960			
UNLESS OTHERWISE SPECIFIED DIMENSIONS ARE IN MILLIMETERS			
DRAWN BY C. MITCHELL	DATE 7-20-84	APPROVED BY	DATE
SHEET 1 OF 1	DO NOT SCALE	SCALE 1 MM = 2 MM	
HANDLE BAR COMP II			
SIZE C	DRAWING NUMBER 252		REVISION

"We made some really sweet custom details, like these sealed bearing cable guide pulleys for the front gear shifter. They're go anodized to match the custom Campagnolo Record triple cran

That top price was the image I wanted however, so we wer also doing some really awesome US bikes with frames from Tom Teesdale and others. The Everest was the $1,35 top-end production bike with Phil Wood hubs and other custom features. The Comp had lighter tubing and it als had a shorter back end and steeper seat tube.

Some of the decisions were just to engage with the elite riders, to get our bikes taken seriously. We used every top-end standard we could, like English threaded bottom brackets and headset dimensions rather than BMX standards because doing so put us in the department of: "Well, this is serious stuff. It's not a kid's bike, it's not a joke, it's a proper bike made the proper way." We had to do that as the guys we were trying to reach were traditional bike shop people, and particularly the highest-end ones. I knew a lot of these guys from my days of racing. East Coast, Midwest – they knew bikes; they knew what they were doing. They were my peers and I had to make a bike that worked for them. We fitted those bikes with super-high-end Edco and Campagnolo headsets and other pro peloton pieces to match, and they were really something else. How they looked was also super-important so we did some awesome custom finishes. They were totally murdered-out bikes with components painted in opaque black; bikes loaded with fully anodized pieces and even some with chrome plated rear stays and forks like classic European road racing bikes.

When we started MountainBikes I really wanted to make
the shop look professional as we were selling a seriously
expensive product, so both Charlie and I wore suits,
even though he really wasn't too happy about it! The ones
we used to wear in the shop were high quality and so
was the Ralph Lauren suit I bought for the first trip to
Japan. They really worked to get us taken seriously by
industry and investors but a normal suit just didn't, well,
'suit' me so I soon started getting my own custom-made.

Wearing tailored suits coincided with when the doors
really started opening for the business. I think if you look
interesting and memorable that's a real help. I've been
called out of the queue at one of the biggest clubs in
Las Vegas just because of the way I've been dressed –
in a Tom Baker suit in Stewart tartan. That suit has got me
into some amazing places and always puts me straight
into the best conversations. Maybe they want me in there,
because I stand out and because I've made an effort.

VE BEEN CALLED OUT OF THE QUEUE AT ONE OF THE BIGGEST CLUBS IN
AS VEGAS JUST BECAUSE OF THE WAY I'VE BEEN DRESSED – A TOM BAKER
UIT IN STEWART TARTAN. THAT SUIT HAS GOT ME INTO SOME AMAZING
LACES AND ALWAYS PUTS ME STRAIGHT INTO THE BEST CONVERSATIONS.

I'd produced some great bikes in Japan in the 1980s and we were pushing ahead with some really radical projects. Gary Fisher Bikes was seen as the most progressive, innovative brand of that time. But changes in the exchange rate meant Japan wasn't profitable for mass production anymore and the technology was moving on fast. After a century of steel frames, bikes like our CR-7, frames from Cannondale and 'fuselages' from Gary Klein were clearly showing that lighter, stiffer TIG welded alloy frames were the future.

Personally I'd been pushing everything really hard for nearly 15 years and I wanted to step back a little, so when I got what seemed like a really great buy-out offer from the Anlen company in Taiwan it seemed like the ideal solution. Unfortunately it didn't take long to realize it was a real bad move; one that dragged me through some of the worst moments of my life and nearly killed off Gary Fisher Bikes entirely.

Taiwan was a totally different environment from Japan both culturally and from a business perspective. The Taiwanese had grown up the hard way and they were tough. I was once out with the guys from Giant, Taiwan's biggest bike producer, and we were talking about all the different kinds of vegetarianism. One of the guys said: "We were vegetarian most of the time when we were growing up, then someone would find a rat and then we weren't." That really put everything into perspective.

I didn't do the due diligence and see how Anlen were treating their other customers either as, looking back, the warning signs were certainly there. Anlen just saw us as a cash cow they could make money from quickly by ramping up manufacture quantity but dropping quality. They also used us a dumping ground for old or faulty pieces. I should have listened to my brother as he didn't trust them right from the start.

LOOKING BACK IT WAS REAL STUPID AS I HAD LOADS OF OTHER OFFERS FROM COMPANIES WHO WOULD HAVE DONE A GREAT JOB FOR US, BUT I WAS JUST NAIVE AND THOUGHT I KNEW BEST.

"Having a blast at the MountainBikes moving party in 1985. It included a bike derby in the basement with Joe Murray, Jeff Koush and Bill Archibald among others"

I was wanting to get back to racing bikes again and as anyone who's ever got in deep at any level will tell you, racing can be seriously distracting if you're not careful. A lot of the reason why the whole Taiwan thing didn't work out was because I was ignoring the business side and concentrating on my racing. I mean I was doing really well, I was racing with the top guys – I used to team up with three-time Tour de France winner Greg LeMond a lot and Kent Bostick, who'd go on to compete in the 1996 Olympics, was my team leader. I was still mostly a domestique – helping my leaders rather than racing for myself – but when I saw my chance I could still turn on the heat. There was a stage race in Arizona called La Vuelta de Bisbee which was a big deal back then. One of the stages was a criterium circuit race round town with a killer steep climb up High School Hill and then a dangerously technical, high speed descent through Old Bisbee. I loved that stage and in 1992 I only just lost out to Olympic gold medalist Alexi Grewal in the final sprint. I was 100% racing and I loved it, loved it, loved it.

We launched the Gary Fisher global racing team in 1991 and that was really strong too. It was actually run out of Italy by our Italian distributors and those guys were crazy. They used to spend so much on publicity and throw these crazy parties too. They'd put on races and there would be a load of Italian celebrities riding in them. I'd land in Firenze and we'd get straight into a helicopter, go up to the event and then just party all week. We never got any trouble either because if the local *Polizia* showed up one of the guys would just get on his phone right away and we'd see the policeman get a call on the radio and suddenly it'd all be OK.

I used to wonder how they lived like this just from importing bikes, but then I suspected they also did a lot of import work with Colombia and Panama. It meant they could hire the best European riders so I wasn't going to ask any awkward questions. Swiss racer Albert Iten was the 1991 world downhill champion. The Italian superstar Paola Pezzo started racing for us in 1992 and she was amazing too. She was on the team for 12 years and while she didn't always win the race, she always won the podium. She was 100% on that, a proper celebrity and people loved her. As well as the racing we were making some really radical bikes like the RS-1 and the Alembic so from a marketing side of things the Gary Fisher brand was doing great.

RACE SUCCESS REALLY BLINDED ME TO WHAT WAS GOING ON IN OTHER PARTS OF THE BUSINESS

The problems didn't take long to surface. We had several containers arrive from Taiwan with frames that had cracked headtubes. When you looked closely there was paint in the cracks too, so it was clear Anlen didn't give a damn about quality – they'd just painted them over and thought we wouldn't notice. We did an E-Stay (Elevated Chainstay) design to get a super-short back end for climbing and stop chain issues but they didn't make the curved seat tube properly so most of them cracked too. We got bikes fitted with previous generation Shimano XT and other out-of-date or lower quality components that we just couldn't sell. It wasn't even like we were getting the bikes for a good deal either. I could have got them made better by Fairly or Giant for 20% cheaper because those guys knew how to get the best deals from other suppliers. But because I had my head buried in racing, I wasn't watching what other people in the business were doing and pretty much whatever could go wrong did go wrong. Our bookkeeper had a breakdown and successfully sued us for $100,000. The next one suddenly vanished with $30,000 in fake cheques.

Some of the decisions I made didn't work out great either. I had the chance to team up with Diatech on their revolutionary Aheadset system but they were using a 1.125in headtube diameter to my 1.25in Evolution design. I was stupid, I was stubborn and I pissed off my trading company so they went into competition with me and won. I don't blame them either – I was being a dick.

174

I DON'T BLAME THEM EITHER — I WAS BEING A DICK.

Fish Issue

When we did team up it was with the legendary Italian brand Cinelli. We made some branded mountain bikes for them and they were really beautiful. We took them to three trade shows but they totally bombed. Nobody wanted them. What people wanted from Cinelli were their classic handlebars, stems, bar tape and sexy ass Italian road bikes – not Taiwanese MTBs. We ended up selling them at 20% cost.

Another time my then-wife Stella was out in Taiwan choosing colors and found this paint that looked a really good purple under the fluorescent lights they had out there. So we had them done and shipped them to Spain and they rejected them because they turned up and when you looked at them in normal light they were pink. If it had been a good pink or a high-end bike which people wanted to stand out more then we maybe could have made it work, but it was just the entry level Montare model and nobody wanted them – it was yet another disaster.

The lowest point was when I had to fire half the employees the day before Thanksgiving 1991. That was heartbreaking but we were in such a bad place the banks just wanted to see if I was strong enough to do what had to be done to keep us afloat. Can you imagine how hard that is, how bad you feel? I just had to say: "You're a good person, you should go somewhere where they'll look after you better."

All I'd wanted to do was a good thing – to get more people out on bikes and having a good time. I did not want all this shit going on. Getting out of the situation with Anlen was hell too. I had to become my own detective to find out what was really going on and basically hold the Taiwanese hostage with my own brand. It still came right down to the wire trying to find someone else to buy the company before if completely bombed or I got cut out completely. I'd learned some very important lessons though, so I made sure I was real careful about the next business partner I got into bed with.

"The CR-7 collaboration with Richard Cunningham was a radical bike as it mixed an alloy front end with a bolted-on rear end"

"The early '90s Montare used an elevated chain stay design to increase tyre clearance despite a super short 15.5in rear end. That design created a bunch of problems though"

"The Prometheus was our titanium mountain bike frame and it was a sweet ride"

"The Advance was our cheapest bike but the straight gauge tubes were so tough that a bunch of people are still riding today 30 years after we introduced it. I know that because they tell me!"

The RS-1 was made in Japan not Taiwan as it was such a sophisticated machine, but it's a great example of how things were going at that time. It was another collaboration, this time with Mert Lawwill. He was a legendary motocross rider and suspension innovator who'd developed a patented parallelogram four bar linkage suspension system for motorbikes. I knew him from working together on TIG welded frames and when he was working with the Koski brothers on the Pro Cruiser back in the klunker days, and he was already working with our racers too.

RS-1 wasn't the first full suspension mountain bike design but it was loaded with some features that made it a way ahead of its time. Mert's suspension was super-sophisticated in the way it tracked smoothly but still pedaled OK. It was pretty smooth as long as you kept everything clean, and we used really big alloy rear stays and a special 14mm axle bolted into place to keep everything stiff. That meant we had to get Campagnolo to make us a custom rear hub though, as well as use a really early Mountain Cycle disc brake because we couldn't fit rim brakes. For the prototypes we used another disc brake on the front with Mert's crazy leading link speedway motorbike-style forks, but production bikes generally had lighter RockShox forks. The bottom bracket was extra wide to give space for the rear stays and we used two skateboard bumpers as suspension dampers so we needed a custom crank axle too.

That whole bike was just nuts and when everything wa[s] working it was a really great ride. The brakes gave us lots of problems though and the Campagnolo MTB gear barely worked. We had to check the exact density of every skateboard bumper we bought too, as different densities made a massive difference to the ride. I still hav[e] the durometer gauge that Mert gave me for checking th[e] bumpers. Despite all that and the fact it weighed over 30lbs – which was really heavy for the time – we had some amazing reviews of the bike and I knew full suspension was going to be the future. Unfortunately it took several years to actually start selling a lot of fu[ll] suspension bikes – Paola Pezzo winning races on our Sugar bike was the tipping point for us – and we actual[ly] lost money on every one of the 750 RS-1s we made.

The Alembic was a development of the RS-1 and use[d] a very similar Lawwill linkage back end and brake set[-] up. The front end was a radical-looking carbon fiber monocoque designed by Stephen Wilde. He was an exotic wood carver who used to make pipes and othe[r] pieces for Jerry Garcia and the Grateful Dead back in the scene days, and it had some real neat details like a[ ] scoop for the bottle cage. His carvings were then mad[e] into carbon by Toray in Japan and it looked sensationa[l] We showed it first in 1992 and it got a huge amount o[f] interest even with a $5,500 price tag – which was insan[e] for that time. We only ever had seven prototypes mad[e] but some of those bikes are still around. The last one I saw listed for sale was in 2017 and it had a starting pric[e] of €15,000.

I was trying to fight my way out of the Taiwanese mess. The distributors already hated us and our dealers started hating us too, but luckily our public image was intact. Riders still loved what we did, still loved the brand and the innovation we stood for with bikes like the CR-7 and the Alembic, but that wasn't going to last for long.

Thankfully while most things seemed totally out of control I knew I had one crucial bit of leverage. I was the signatory on all the loans from Nissho Iwai, the big Japanese trading company that was bankrolling the whole Taiwanese setup. That meant that, for Anlen to carry on, I either had to remain on the payroll, or they had to get rid of me – which meant a payoff and the freedom to grab the Fisher name back. So I went in hard. I told them I wanted them my salary doubling. Since I was already on good money, this was asking for a lot. Especially when things were so bad that we were selling a lot of our bikes at or even below cost.

They knew what I was doing too. They sent one of their guys up, his name was Sid Dunofsky, and he was a proper heavy, an ex-boxer, a physically scary dude. In time we actually wound up getting along really well and laughing about this whole situation later on but back then he was furious. He came into this meeting in this sharp Italian suit and he's shouting:

"GARY, WHAT DO YOU THINK YOU'RE DOING ?
YOU'RE HOLDING A GUN TO OUR HEADS , YOU CAN'T DO THIS ,
YOU'RE GOING TO BRING THE WHOLE THING DOWN."

SO I SAY TO HIM:

"DUDE, I'VE HAD A GUN HELD TO MY HEAD
AND THIS IS NOTHING LIKE THAT."

And I tell him this whole story about the time back in the scene when I was round my friend's house. He was a dealer and we got raided by another deal and his crew. They burst in, beat us down and tied us up on the floor and the they literally put a gun right in my face and said: "OK, you need to tell us where the dope is and where the money is right now." That was some scary shit, mar I will never forget that, but right then it was good enough to show Sid he wasn going to scare me. So I went one stage further: I told him that if he didn't agree to double my salary right then then I'd add $5k for every day they delayed. Man h was pissed when he left. It took them three days to finally agree to the new salary, so they had to add an extra $15k too.

I knew they'd be looking for ways to get rid of me as soon as they could though and luckily they weren't so great at hiding it. Their plan was to tell Nissho Iwai – the Japanese investment compa[ ] – that I'd brought the value of the Fisher brand down so much that it was dead as a prestige bra[ ] They could then sell the name to Howie Cohen at West Coast Cycles, who was one of the first g[ ] to ever bring bikes in from Asia. He was the importer of Kuwahara and Nishiki BMXes and he ha[ ] made an absolute fortune because he had the license for the bike from the film ET. Howie and th[ ] Taiwanese were going to set up a totally new low-cost, low-quality operation down in Los Angele[ ] and just planned to wring the last dollars out of the Fisher name until it was totally dead.

FISHER MOUNTAINBIKES

140 Mitchell Blvd.
San Rafael, CA 94903
415/479-1880
Telex # 493860
Fax # 1-415-479-1888

Gary Fisher
President

BICYCLING

A RODALE PRESS PUBLICATION
33 E. MINOR ST., EMMAUS, PA 18049
215-967-5171

Gary Fisher
ASSOCIATE EDITOR

HOME: 91 MONO ST.
FAIRFAX, CA 9[ ]
415-453-7[ ]

GARY FISHER
PRESIDENT

Middle Peak.

GARY FISHER BICYCLE COMPANY
140 MITCHELL BLVD. SAN RAFAEL, CALIFORNIA 94903
415/479/1880   FAX 415/479/8240

GARY C. FISHER
SENIOR MEN
50-11-05
VELO CLUB TAMALPAIS

LIC. NUMBER M01188
DISTRICT 01
COLOURS

S
H
B
EGORY 1

USCF
UNITED STATES
1978 05956 S
CYCLING FEDERATION

EXPIRES
DEC. 31, 1978
USCF REG. OFFICE
BOX 480
EAST DETROIT, MI 48021

ATTACH PHOTO
HERE FOR
INTERNATIONAL
LICENSE

SIGNATURE OF HOLDER

MOUNTAIN BIKES
P.O. Box 405
Fairfax, CA 94930
(415) 456-1898

GARY FISHER

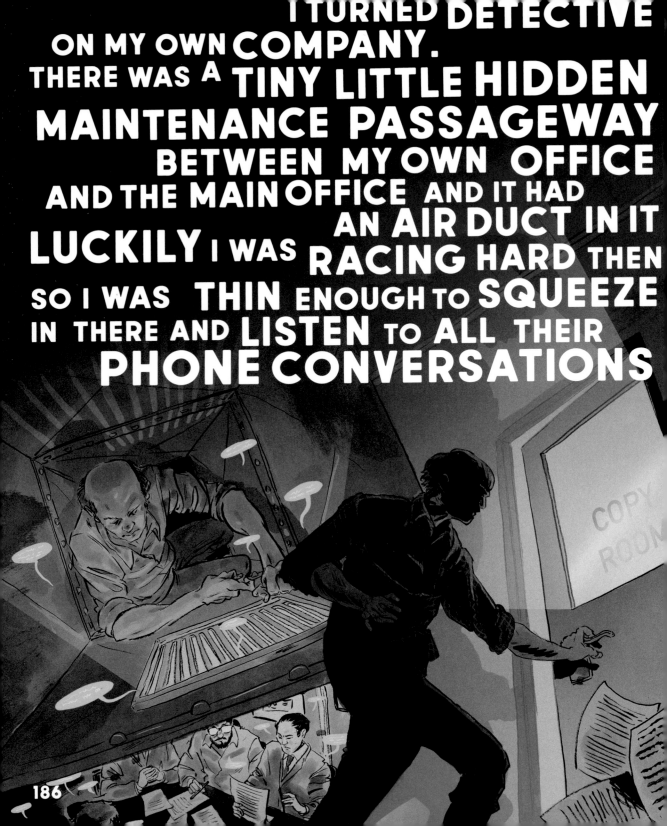

We also had a fax machine in the office and they used that to send a lot of the documents and proposed deals back and forth. Obviously they used to get rid of all the printouts and scans they'd sent or received, but they forgot the machine had a memory, so every night I used to wait until they went home and print them all out again.

So I knew everything that was going on, and after the stunt I'd pulled I wasn't surprised they were doing it, but I was scared as shit. I was going to lose the brand; I was going to lose everything I'd worked so hard on for so long and I was going to lose my living. I had to do something real quick but this time I wasn't going to jump straight in with someone and make an even bigger mistake. This time I was going to be careful who I got into bed with. The trouble was that all the offers I'd had so far just sounded like even more of a big mess. I was just handing them on to Howie to keep him busy – he was basically acting as a liquidator at that point so he had to give every deal a good look. The one I didn't hand over to Howie, however, was the approach I got from Trek.

A BIG DIESEL ENGINE, NOT A HOT ROD BLOCK LIKE WE WERE.

I'd written a story about Trek for *Bicycling* magazine a few years before. I gave it the title "A giant is growing in the Midwest" and that was how most people saw them as a brand. A big diesel engine, not a hot rod block like we were. They'd started in 1976 as an offshoot of a domestic goods distributor where Dick Burke worked. He'd gotten into cycling on a trip to Italy and at that time bike sales were still strong in the US from the oil crisis. So when he came back the company gave him some money to start building steel touring frames in a barn in Wisconsin.

Trek hadn't been doing anything particularly exciting but what they did do, they did really well. In 1982 – when I was going through a super-tough patch trying to make US manufacturing work, buried in a ton of debt and desperately waiting for my Japanese-built bikes to arrive – Trek had already had a proper bike building plant up and running in Wisconsin for three years. They were already making mountain bikes as well as touring and racing bikes and they had a turnover of $20 million.

Compared to what we were doing their image was definitely a little dull, and before I came on board they only had two people in their marketing department. I've been in enough relationships to know that your best partner is never your mirror image though, and I figured we both had something that the other needed and that could be a recipe for a really good marriage. I really liked those guys too, and I still do, which is pretty crazy after all we've been through together since then.

As soon as I get the approach from Dick and John Burke, I jump straight on a plane to Wisconsin where they're based and we meet up at this hotel. Not at the Trek company campus, just at this hotel in Madison, so nobody knows I'm even there or that these talks are taking place. And I'm selling hard, because man I'm literally selling for my life here and even though things were going to shit with Fisher I had some great data on the brand. We got hold of this survey from *Bicycling* magazine which said we were still the most popular mountain bike brand with riders and we were the brand most riders said they wanted to buy next. That was pretty amazing considering what was going on behind the scenes. By the end of that day Trek were on board.

I already knew a meeting had been arranged between Howie, his Japanese ally Taka Nayada and the guys from Nissho Iwai where they're going to cut me out completely and start the new company. But of course they don't know I know this is going down, so you can imagine their faces when I walk into the meeting, with Dick Burke, and say: "Great news, Trek are going to buy the company!" The Japanese guys were absolutely delighted because suddenly their investment was saved and even though Howie was totally pissed when it happened he did more than OK with West Coast Cycles once we'd paid him out. He was a lot older than me and sadly he passed away a few years ago, but we used to meet up and we'd have a laugh about how crazy things got back then.

And that was that, on April 3rd 1992 – and that's a date I'll always remember – I went from nearly losing everything I'd built up to joining forces with one of the biggest bike players in the US. Trek had our back and Fisher was back on track.

The funny thing was they were actually benefiting from the increasing amount of imports. Schwinn were still a big deal in the mass market and they wouldn't let their dealers stock any brand with Japanese links as they saw it as direct competition. They were happy if their guys stocked Trek though as the bikes were good quality and priced higher than anything that Schwinn made, so there was no conflict.

Trek intrigued me. Ever since I wrote that feature I'd been watching them – and they had some bad patches. Even they would admit they didn't seem to have a real plan for a long time. But when Dick Burke took over full control in 1985 he got them sorted, and with his son John having joined the company they just kept growing and growing. They were a good team, they were traditional but they were ambitious and proud of what they did. They did sales team football chants and when they had a good month they'd share out champagne and cigars on the shop floor. At Trek nobody goes home until the last customer is happy and it's always been like that. If something goes wrong nobody points a finger; everyone just wants to sort the problem out and turn it into a success. They worked as a team to make that happen and they had the resources to back it up. They were (and still are) just really honorable guys doing a really good, solid job.

I DIDN'T MIND. I WAS REALLY GOOD AT THOSE THINGS, I WAS EXACTOMUNDO.

192

I really had to hit the ground running at Trek though. Not least because I was on a big bonus if I got the new Fisher bikes up and running ready for the '93 season. And when I first went to Trek I was still doing everything. Frame design, component choices. I even knew all the part numbers. I did the price negotiation with the vendors and everything – I still loved that whole process.

The difference at Trek was what I wanted to happen did happen because they had the muscle. So I took Harry Spehar and John Bradley, the Trek product managers, and we hit up all my suppliers, factories and vendors in Japan and Taiwan and we totally nailed it. I really liked those guys. You gotta remember I hadn't laughed in a long time, but we traveled all over to get the job done and we had a really good time.

Those guys in Asia were also super-keen to deal now that we had proper backing and we made things happen. Looking back now it seems crazy just how well such a massive change went but I was on a total mission and the transition was real smooth.

I worked in a different way to how Trek always had. Harry and John used to do all the spec choices on the bikes and liaise with the Asian suppliers to get them sorted out. Then Dick would go over and try and force them down on price. The vendors knew they already had the order and it would be difficult to change so they never moved much on price. I never used to fix the spec until I'd got the price right down. That way you could play vendors off against each other and because they didn't want to lose the business you'd get the best deals. As a result we didn't just get that range for the '93 season in on time – we got it in early and on price. John and Dick were delighted and I got my bonus.

That first range had some carry over of existing designs such as the RS-1 and Procaliber, but being at Trek meant I also got to play with a whole new bunch of options. In the first year we had 10 new bikes based on US-made steel and alloy frames and that even included cheaper steel versions of the RS-1, which we called Expert. The second year I used a rebadged version of Trek's super-light OCLV carbon fiber frame and built it into the Procaliber LTD. I went full out and threw everything from our race team arsenal at that bike. We went crazy. The RockShox forks had a titanium hop up kit, we had a titanium Syncros seatpost, a carbon fiber Bontrager saddle, Grafton brakes and cranks, White Industries hubs. It was totally tricked out in the lightest, money-no-object kit available and the whole bike weighed just over 20lbs. We put it on the first spread of the catalog and that properly shook things up. I think it shook Trek up too as the equivalent bike in their line was nearly three pounds (1.3kg) heavier and had a Trek-branded Showa fork that nobody wanted, so it was a disaster compared to ours. They actually took that frame off us in the end because they said having both brands using it was confusing to buyers and OCLV was their technology. That was the official reason, anyway, but I think they were just getting heat from their dealers that we were building a better bike. That was after we'd already won a world championship and the first Olympic MTB gold medal on it though, so it had definitely done its work for us.

I was still super-keen to leverage racing to push the Gary Fisher brand but it certainly wasn't an easy sell at first. Trek had a couple of top 10 national racers in Travis Brown and Don Myrah but in general their policy was totally anti-race and anti-team as they had a very simple view on the economics involved. They used to tell dealers: "We don't have a race team because they cost a lot of money. Do you want us to have one and raise our prices?" Of course all the dealers would just go: "No! No!" Like I say, they'd only had two people working on the marketing for the whole company and they never thought about the positive impact a successful race team and publicity could have on their sales.

But I kept the Fisher racing team going and, in 1992, brought the Italian national champion Paola Pezzo on board too. In under a year she'd won the world championships. The publicity we got from that was incredible and totally changed Trek's minds about racing teams.

"The Grateful Dead bike was a standard '95 Hoo Koo E Koo with skeletal graphic decals by GD artist Prairie Prince and Tioga 'butterscotch' tyres. Try and buy one (with the matching T-shirt) now though and you'd best have around $10,000 spare!"

Paola was so awesome, the ultimate package. She was sexy as hell when she wanted to be and sh undeniably grabbed attention with those famous pictures with her unzipped top and the silver lam Castelli skin shorts at the 1996 Atlanta Olympics. But she was also a good Catholic girl at heart, an she was totally dedicated with her training and he racing. She was a real fighter too. She crashed at the Atlanta Olympic race – the first time mountair biking had ever been included in the Games – bu got back on and fought back to win by over a minute That was amazing for us, to not just win the first MTB Olympic gold medal but at an Olympics hosted in America. I was actually on stage in a big sales presentation in Santa Cruz and Dick Burke walked up on to the stage and told me she'd won the gold That was a magic moment and she won every rac she started for over a year after that as well.

The response was incredible, not just in the US bu across the whole world. She worked hard as hell fo it though. Wherever she was, Paola would just go out and own the course completely, just ride it unt she was just totally confident with every part of it. Her value wasn't just about being the fastest ever time either. Even if she didn't win she always had perfect timing for the podium. She'd be deliberate late so people were shouting for her and the camer were all waiting and she'd rock up in a killer outfit every time. She had it nailed.

Gary Fisher
SUGAR DADDY

49 Karl Ave. San Anselmo, Ca. 94960
415·459-5570 Fax:415·459-6001
e·mail: geefisher@aol.com

Sales were going great and we combined our separate Trek and Fisher sales forces so we became more efficient. We could get better deals from suppliers this way because together we were buying on a much bigger scale and we were a super-important customer to vendors so we had some real clout. I had some really good people in my team as well – product and brand manager guys like Joe Vadeboncoeur and Aaron Mock – so I didn't have to do the day-to-day micro-managing. That freed up a whole load of time so I could just concentrate on new ideas, like the Joshua full suspension bike in 1996.

The Joshua was a properly neat piece of design that's still copied today because it was so simple. Trek already had their carbon fiber 'Y' frame bike but they showed me some really complicated initial drawings for the suspension bike they thought I should make with Fisher. Instead I just drew my own version of the Y design on a piece of scrap paper in a flat minute. It joined up the three crucial attachment points for the handlebars, saddle and cranks with just two super-sized oval tubes. Because it had very few pieces and very little weld seam length it was really easy and fast to put together. And it was a massive billboard too – we could write our name on that frame real big! We even made a BMX version and a freeride version called Level Betty. That name always used to crack me up, it was a name I heard from my sister-in-law. Just some story about what she'd called her trailer park neighbor when she was carrying a massive bag of groceries in each hand. I've used names from all over the place over the years but I still laugh every time I think about that one.

197

I raced it on a hand built, steel framed bike that w
a prototype for a new bike geometry and I won t.
40+ category even though I was closer to 50 tha
40 at the time. I got on the Lufthansa flight back ho
and one of the flight crew had seen me winning an
he said "I'm a really big fan, your win was amazir
you're going first class" and they upgraded me on
spot! That's the kind of crazy shit that racing car
do in terms of recognition – and not just in specia
media, but everywhere. With that and with Paola a
our other racers smashing it up on the race scer
the sales in Europe just exploded.

The funniest thing about that race was that ther
was no way we could have sold the bike I won o
Genesis Geometry started like most of my ideas
trying to solve a problem I kept having when ridir
– handling.

Having good people and good process was giving
me time to design bikes and do marketing – the two
things I was best at. Truthfully though, the best part
was that it also gave me the chance to ride my
bike a lot more again, to get some peace and calm
– which I hadn't had for a long time. It gave me a
chance to get fit and get back into some racing too,
which was so good. I won the master category of
the national XC championships in 1997 and actually
made the team for the masters world championships.
I had an even bigger goal for 1998 though – the
TransAlp Challenge.

1998 was the first year of the event and it had already
been massively hyped in Europe. All of our dealers
and distributors over there were going mad about
it. It's a seven-day mountain bike stage race across
the Alps from Germany to Italy and it's a real monster.
370 miles (595km) long with 60,000ft (18,500m)
of climbing and descending. I'd done a bunch of
stage races on the road before but nothing like that
off-road. It was the perfect opportunity to combine
my three favorite things: marketing, racing, and trying
out a new bike idea.

Sure, mountain bike handling wasn't quite as crazy as it was back in the early '90s when they were basically road bikes with fat tires and flat bars and John Tomac was using a 73° head angle and 6in (150mm) stems and 23in (580mm) handlebars. By the late '90s steering had gotten a bit slacker, stems a bit shorter and bars a bit wider. But the basic shape of bikes hadn't changed since we'd introduced the Procaliber a decade before. Even with suspension and other advances meaning we were going a lot faster, the handling hadn't been updated. I was out riding and maybe I'm having a bad day anyway but the bike sure isn't helping and I go over the bars a couple of times. So I'm sat on the ground just thinking: "You know, this is all stupid; I can't steer properly, the stem is too long to react fast enough to trouble and the wheelbase is too short and unstable." So I convinced the higher-ups to let me try something different again and started experimenting.

We ended up building around 50 bikes with slightly different geometries over a couple of years and, like always, I had to try some things on the outside edges. The TransAlp bike was one of those. It was custom made by Doug Cusack, who was one of the engineers at Trek and a really great framebuilder. It had short 15.5in/395mm chain stays which gave it incredible traction. You could get in and out of the saddle at will. But the Shimano minimum recommended length was 415mm, otherwise the chain was operating at too much of an angle and so there was a real issue with gear shifting on that bike. It was OK under power but it would fall straight off if you back pedaled, so there was no way we could put it into production.

We found a good compromise between better handling and a workable chain line in the end though and it got people thinking about geometry again. If I look back over my whole life that's probably what I'm proudest of overall, not just one specific thing but just making people think about stuff. I'm not a genius or anything, in fact I'd always rather be the dumbest person in the room as that way you're sure to learn something. I've never been afraid to put myself out there and see what happens though and it's awesome when that helps other people follow their dreams and ideas.

IF I LOOK BACK OVER MY WHOLE LIFE THAT'S PROBABLY WHAT I'M PROUDEST OF OVERALL NOT JUST ONE SPECIFIC THING BUT JUST MAKING PEOPLE THINK ABOUT STUFF I'M NOT A GENIUS IN FACT I'D ALWAYS OR ANYTHING RATHER BE THE DUMBEST PERSON IN THE ROOM AS THAT WAY YOU'RE SURE TO LEARN SOMETHING

Being innovative and inventive attracts the best people. Carl Matson, the Trek engineer who headed up the Speed Concept Aero bike project, was a Navy aircraft composites engineer and a world class age group triathlete. In the Navy he was working with some really cool, advanced stuff but he couldn't actually use the things he was developing or take them home. With bikes he gets to work with a similar level of technology but he gets to use them at the weekend. It's very rare that happens with really high level, groundbreaking technology.

We did some crazy stuff with colors and design too. When we were preparing to release the first production 29in wheel mountain bikes in 2000, it was a real big break from the norm. I wanted to do something special to engage the media so we arranged to race at 24-hour relay races in different countries. They were a big deal at the time and we made the teams up with influential journalists from each country and they'd ride our prototype big-wheeled bikes. I wanted to have a really stand out look for the bikes and the team clothing, so everyone knew something different was going down.

I'd been a friend and big fan of the English clothes designer Paul Smith for a long time. He's a super-keen cyclist and he used to make suits for me so I always used to see him when I was in London. I asked Paul to help and he did a version of his classic candy pinstripe design to use on the frame tubes and the jerseys and they just looked awesome. They still look great today and they're real collectors' pieces now.

I was lucky that Trek gave me so much freedom. The whole Paul Smith collaboration came from me and Brian Buckle, who was the marketing guy in the UK at that time, and we totally wrote our own ticket on it. I was pretty pushy with Trek. I'd go over to Wisconsin from California and I'd go see the higher-ups and just read them the riot act and say: "Look, you're going to do this or you're going to die." Luckily they were a lot more innovative and open-minded than many people gave them credit for and they backed me up a surprising amount of times.

"We had a ton of fun at Trek, even remaking a klunker with state of the art components, nothing was off-limits!"

There was a whole lot of other stuff that we trialed with Gary Fisher but which ended up being adopted by Trek for their own bikes too. 29er wheels was obviously the big one, but the DRCV shocks we developed with Fox Racing Shox were another. The softail suspension frame we made for Paola Pezzo which she won her second Olympic Gold medal on was actually released as a Trek bike – the STP – rather than as a Gary Fisher as we'd developed the Sugar full suspension race bike at the same time. Genesis Geometry, carbon fiber flex stays on suspension bikes, big volume tires, disc brakes – they all appeared on our bikes first too before being adopted by Trek.

Having different bikes for each brand eventually became a major pain in the ass, so in 2010 Trek renamed our range 'The Gary Fisher Collection by Trek'. I'll be honest that was a real surprise when they sprung that on me at Euro-bike, but I got it. Then a couple of years later I was down in Australia and saw bikes and they didn't even have my name on them anymore. In all honesty I was fucking pissed at the time, I was thinking I'm gonna lose my job, but it's actually worked out really well. I still work with the product guys on some projects because I really enjoy it and actually if you look at the bikes in the Trek line up now there's still a whole lot of Gary Fisher in them. More importantly they've given me the opportunity to travel all over the world, following a much bigger dream of a better cycling future and giving other people permission to follow their dreams too. That's the really exciting part of my story and it's where we're headed next.

29ERS

Besides starting MountainBikes, the biggest thing people know me for is popularizing the 29in wheel for mountain bikes. It's now the dominant size in nearly all parts of dirt riding but 20 years ago it was a real fight to convince people to even try it.

Again, it wasn't anything new, nowhere near. 100 years ago 28 and 32in wheels were the most common sizes. The only reason we'd adopted 26in in the first place was because it was convenient. It's what the cruiser bikes we were modding came with and 95% of US bike shops had a Uniroyal knobby 26x2in tire for $11.95. As far back as the '70s I remember sitting at the top of Pearl Pass above Crested Butte discussing wheel size with Charlie Cunningham (who became one of the founders of bike and component company Wilderness Trail Bikes – WTB). The trails up in Colorado were really rocky, way rockier than back in Marin. Some were as big as the 26in wheels on our klunkers. I can remember us saying: "You know, if we used a bigger wheel, that would just roll over stuff so much better."

It just made sense, because you look at bikes from further back in history and they had all kinds of sizes of wheels. Anyway, Charlie and I talked about it a bunch on and off over the years but there was always something else to fix or try out instead.

Other people were making bigger wheeled mountain bikes well before we even started experimenting with them at Fisher Bikes – in fact that was part of the problem. Some of those guys were real evangelists and they were ringing the editors over and over again telling them big wheels were going to be the future and giving them a really hard time when they were skeptical. They were sounding like total cranks and it was turning the really influential people off the whole idea when they should have been totally turned on to it.

Anyway I was talking to the guys at WTB in the late '90s – they were our tire suppliers and sponsors for the race team – and the whole question of wheel size came up again. And I said: "You know, why are we just talking about this every time we meet up. Why aren't we actually checking it out? Getting out there and seeing what works and what doesn't?"

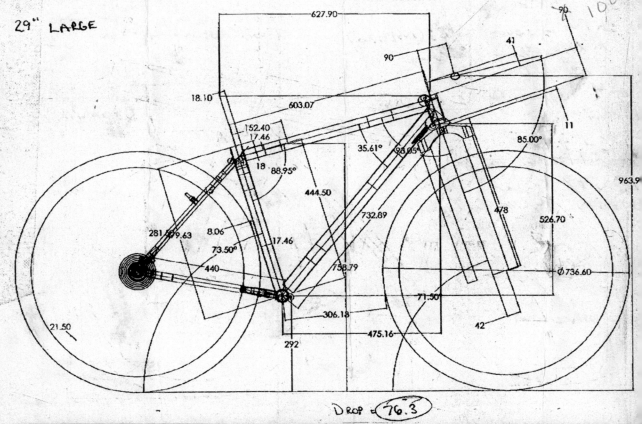

re molds are expensive so I had to put my money where
y mouth was. I personally paid for them to make me a
old for a 29er version of their Nano Raptor tire. It was
e tire design we used the most and so we knew exactly
ow it performed in different conditions. Then we made
29er frame as well as a conventional 26in frame with
close as possible the same geometry. We equipped
em as identically as we could and I put a heart rate
onitor on to gauge my efforts and got my timing gear
ut. I rode them round as many different tracks as I could,
ack to back over and over again. In the end we made
different 29er prototypes with slight changes to each
e to see what worked and what didn't. The funny thing
– and not many people know this – I even made five
.5in wheeled bikes at the same time just to check that
ut as an option.

What I learned was that even though the heavier,
bump-shrinking wheels felt slower because they didn't
accelerate as quick and the trail buzz was reduced,
the 29er was actually faster pretty much everywhere.
Downhill, climbing, even on pavement. Everywhere I
tested it was around 5% faster and it was smoother and
gripped better on climbs too. I was like: "Wow, this thing
really is better! Noticeably, provably, significantly faster
and with more control." The more I rode the more I began
to appreciate how much it saved energy over time too,
by effectively shrinking all the bumps on the trail and
sustaining speed better from increased inertia.

There was still a lot to do though. Tires and wheels were pretty easy but the first suspension forks we had from Marzocchi were just stretched versions of their normal forks. That reduced the overlap between the upper and lower tubes and they flexed so much that if you braked too hard it forced the fork legs apart and basically locked them solid.

Even once we had a bike that worked, there was a lot of resistance. Because 29ers looked different people didn't want to try them and because they felt smooth rather than fast you only realized how quick you were going if you rode with your normal buddies and beat them. It was like the early klunker times all over again and it was even some of the same people giving me shit! I guess some people just don't like mixing things up like I do.

Another problem in the early days was that back then 29ers were actually illegal for racing at the highest level. That's a big issue when you're designing a race bike to win world cup, world championship and Olympic races! The UCI, the governing body that sets all the rules for cycle racing globally, had put a 26in wheel maximum limit on mountain bikes. They were worried that if they allowed bigger wheels people would race cyclo-cross bikes on their courses not mountain bikes. I went over to Switzerland twice to lobby them and my argument was pretty simple. While freeriders were hucking off massive cliffs and DH courses were getting really technical, cross-country mountain bike courses hadn't changed at all. That meant bikes hadn't changed either. So I said: "If you don't want people riding 'cross bikes, then stop making courses that suck! Make proper mountain bike courses that you can't ride on a 'cross bike!"

Eventually in 2003 the UCI changed the rules and when they did I was so happy. I'd worked so hard and finally it was all coming together. I was so excited I took my 29er and I went charging out up Mount Tam, where we used to run the Repack. I was going so fast, I was invincible, nothing could stop me, it was awesome. Right up to the point where I crashed and broke my wrist. You gotta laugh about moments like that though. Sometimes the world has a way of literally bringing you back down pretty hard when you're getting too carried away with yourself.

You know what was interesting about 29ers too? It wasn't the flagship race bikes that made people c to bigger wheels. We still had a lot of resistance from racers because bigger wheels and tires and longer fo were heavier and those guys are serious weight weeni I mean we nearly gave the whole idea up. We had tw 29er bikes in our 2002 line up, six in 2003, but just thr in 2004. It looked like the whole idea had been anoth expensive too much, too soon gamble.

The bike that made it click for riders was this super-simple single gear machine called the Rig. Singlespee bikes were a cult item around then and the Rig was cheap and it looked real clean, so a bunch of people wh had heavy full suspension bikes bought them as their second bike. What they found though was that when th rode it they weren't just keeping up with their buddies they were beating them. I used to meet riders and ge letters saying: "Hey, I was the back of the bunch dude now I'm leading them out. I'm kicking their ass on climb and I'm dropping them on descents. This bike is crazy, thanks so much man!"

I love moments like that. It was like watching people on their first Larkspur rides or coming back to the MountainBikes shop with this wild look in their wide eye You know they've got it now and you've given them something awesome. That's truly the best feeling in the world and bikes are a wonderful way to give that gift. Bikes really are the happiest invention in the world.

My good friend Paul Smith has made me a few suits, including a grey one and this red velvet one with yellow laser cut flowers. Edward Sexton has also made me a suit. He took four sittings to get it right, but the fit is immaculate. Tailors seem to love making suits for cyclists because we have the best asses!

You can tell a lot about a market by the way people dress. You can even work out what bike colours will sell into different countries by just going online and seeing what slacks they sell in the popular stores. If they sell coloured slacks then you can sell colorful bikes – it's as simple as that!

I've been part of some amazing movements in the 70 years I've been around. The scene and mountain bikes both created totally new ways to free your mind and challenge boundaries in a profoundly life-changing way.

I'm really proud of that but I'm not satisfied at all. How can I be? We're choking where we live. Poisoning where our kids play and letting them get so unhealthy their life expectancy is less than ours. How can we be satisfied with that?

As cyclists our duty, our challenge, is now changing how people get around cities and waking people up to how awesome their bodies and environments could be. That isn't going to be easy, but it just comes down to selling something you truly believe in and that's something I have a lot of experience in.

I've watched others change the way people live and behave, many times. Look at how the organic food movement started. When my grandpa used to take me to farmers markets the stuff looked horrific. Oh man, it was like a vegetable horror show, bizarrely-shaped carrots and mangled-looking potatoes. But as soon as people tried it they realized how much better it tasted and how good eating clean food makes you feel. Now suppliers are much more aware of the aesthetic and it's much better presented, but what really helped was getting chefs interested. 'Farm to fork' was adopted by high-end restaurants looking for a way to stand out, and eating clean and eating organic suddenly became a status symbol – not just something social outcast hippies did. That's starting to happen with bikes too, but we really have to push it and exploit it if we're going to change things.

IF YOU'RE IN A TOWN OR A CITY, JUST GO OUTSIDE. STAND NEXT TO THE TRAFFIC, SMELL THE POLLUTION. TASTE IT ON YOUR TONGUE. IT'S POISON , MAN.

Some places are already way ahead of others with changing attitudes to bike use, but let's start with the basic fundamentals like the language we use. Have you seen those slogans on road signs? "You're not stuck in traffic, you ARE traffic!" It's such a powerful message – a really strong flip round that makes people think exactly when they're at their most motivated to make a change. That's how to do it right. We've also got to stop referring to traffic 'accidents' too. Accidents happen, but traffic crashes are problems caused by dangerous streets, unsafe vehicles and drivers who either don't think enough or just don't care – and that's all fixable. In the Netherlands if there's an incident involving a bike and a car, the presumed liability is always with the motorist so drivers are a lot more careful and considerate. So let's flip that emphasis on who should be protected, stop using the word accident and start treating these deaths and injuries seriously. Today

It's a devastating fact that most cyclists know someone who has been killed when riding a bike. We're not going to make people want to ride bikes if they think they're going to die, so above all we need to create a safer, enjoyable cycling environment. My wife is a doctor, who rides a bike to get around. She's not a racer or a fanatic but she loves riding her bike on her own or with me or with the whole family – but only if she feels safe. If a route doesn't feel safe she's not going to go on it, and she certainly isn't going to bring the kids. The Dutch have got it right here again though, they totally understand the importance of flow to making cycling safe and enjoyable for everyone. Dutch cyclists have right of way over cars at intersections too, so there's no interruption of their journey. But in most of the world 'bike lanes' are these little sections that are too narrow and swerve on and off roads and sidewalks and, oh man, that completely kills the flow.

EVERY LESSON I'VE LEARNED IN CYCLING AND LIFE

HAS TAUGHT ME THAT FLOW IS CENTRAL TO EVERYTHING.

nding the rhythm in your first paceline. Working together so you're taking turns to beat the wind or make a
eak from the pack. We started riding klunkers because they smoothed out the trails we wanted to explore.
en we fitted gears to them so we could carry on pedaling and make the climbs as much fun as the
scents. We went to Japan to get our bikes built because trying to scratch together builds from all over the
ace was killing us. We changed geometry so we could carry speed through corners better. We added
spension to float over rocks. The whole reason I worked so hard to get 29er bikes going was because
ling over rough stuff was what they did best and made the whole experience so much easier. Whatever
u're doing, improving the flow and finding a smooth rhythm is key to making cycling fun.

e already know how to make bike ways that are really good fun to ride. Paths that make you feel great,
ve you a real buzz while managing the speed and safety aspects really well, already exist off-road.
ountain bike trail builders have got the geometry for that down superbly. They think in 3D not 2D and
ey build everything around flow. Places like Ray's Indoor Mountain Bike Park in Cleveland, Ohio, are aiming
r fun without being risky and they pack in an amazing amount of riders and skill levels into a tiny space
thout any issue. We just have to translate that concept and design language into an urban transport setting.

here are already some places, like Eagle and Fruita in Colorado, where urban pump track sidewalks
e part of routes to schools and they are awesome, for several reasons. For a start, because these flow
aths are fun to use, people actually use them. They also require balance and fitness, they're the whole
ognitive deal, a rolling mental and physical gym. That means the kids using them to get to school arrive
witched on and ready to go.

RAPID TRANSIT ACROSS GOLDEN GATE . . .
Plans call for the span's value to the entire
Bay Area to be further enhanced by addition
of this new, convenient, high-speed facility.

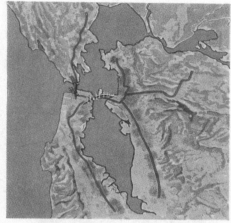

213

Flow works on the street too. Coned-off lanes for social distancing during the Covid-19 lockdown showed that a little extra space makes a big difference to how easy it is for people to move around. They retime stop lights in Chicago to match bike speeds and the average cycling speed went up from six to 10mph. They're now doing the same in New York and calling it the 'green wave' because you surf from one sign on green to the next. That also brings average traffic speeds below the point at which hitting a cyclist or a pedestrian is likely to be fatal.

Bikes shouldn't just be seen in isolation either. In South Korea they've completely repurposed major roads. They've put bike paths in the middle of freeway systems and they've roofed them with solar panel. They spent some real money and they're having real results. So many people are using them it's amazing. In Singapore they allowed folding bikes on all transport so people could get further to and from bus and train stations without a car. People got so into riding and the obvious benefits of it they then built mounta bike trails around the city to make recreational riding easier and more fun. That's two very separate side of cycling synced side-to-side for a double win effect.

BUSES ↓ ONLY

215

These relatively small, practical changes in infra-
structure can make a real difference. But that doesn't
mean we shouldn't think big and maybe even a little
crazy to really get things moving.

I mean, come on, why just fight for a single lane on
the Golden Gate Bridge when we could put a whole
pedestrian and cycling deck underneath it?
Why fight for space on the streets with cars, why
not take bike lanes into a whole new dimension?
That's another 3D lesson we can learn from
mountain biking. The North Shore area in Vancouver
was basically unrideable because the forest floor
was so covered in fallen trees and debris. So what
did the freeriders do? They built this whole freaking
elevated trail network with jumps and drops
and see-saws and all this crazy shit way up in the
trees. It was so different that every magazine and
filmmaker wanted a piece of it and soon every
damn wood in the world had some kids building
these North Shore-style trails. They overcame their
environment, created something that captured the
imagination and inspired a total shift in the riding
scene.

It'd be really easy to do something like that in cities,
safely and on a really big scale. Even before North
Shore we had a drawing in our 1994 Fisher catalog
showing this future city with fully enclosed over-
head tunnels for bikes. Then it turns out that an
architect called Chris Hardwicke had also proposed
something very similar in Toronto and called it
Velo-City. I thought, wow, someone else is thinking
about this. Now that sort of idea is all over Zwift
with these fantasy virtual cycling worlds. You go on
the New York world and you're riding these tunnels
and skyways through the city. You can see how
amazing it could be, even when you're pedaling a
stationary bike while staring at a computer screen.

Elevated bike ways would work really well because
they're quiet and clean – not like an elevated train
or roadway that creates all this noise and pollution.
Fully enclosed paths would also totally separate
riders from the traffic and protect them from the
weather. That's two of the biggest obstacles that
stop more people riding removed right there. It
would be really easy to design them with venting that
creates directional airflow so there's a permanent
tailwind. You don't have to have many riders heading
in the same direction to boost that airflow even
more until you're absolutely flying.

IT COULD ALSO MAKE THE SECOND STORIES OF BUILDINGS A LOT MORE USEFUL TOO . HAVE YOU SEEN HOW MANY SECOND FLOORS IN CITIES ARE DESERTED OR JUST LOOK LIKE THEY'RE FULL OF JUNK IF WE COMBINED BETTER BIKE FACILITIES ON THE GROUND AND THEN LINKED TO THESE 'VELODUCTS' EVERY FEW BLOCKS – LIKE A BIKE INTERSTATE – YOU COULD HAVE THIS AMAZINGLY EFFICIENT AND EASY BIKE-BASED TRANSIT SYSTEM

Getting people onto bikes or moving around on foot isn't just great for reducing pollution and noise. It's also great for regenerating local business and breathing life back into neighborhoods. Bike riders and pedestrians are more likely to use local bakeries, coffee shops, restaurants and markets because they can literally smell the good stuff. They can stop and buy stuff on impulse, without needing to find a parking space too. In 2012 the New York City Department of Trade published evidence on the impact of work to create streets that are friendlier to cyclists and pedestrians. On Ninth Avenue, where a protected bike lane was created, there had been a 49% rise in trade – borough wide for the same time period, the figure was only 3%. In Münster, Germany's most cycle friendly city, a city survey found that because people were visiting the main street shops more frequently they weren't only buying more but were buying more fresh produce – so that's boosting their health benefits even further.

Trek is spending a huge amount of time and money on campaigning and pushing the agenda and they've got some real political power behind them. They're successful and they're solid. It's a good old-fashioned American business who the folks in power understand and identify with. Never underestimate the influence that can have as we're getting some real momentum on all this now. Politicians all over the world are starting to take notice. I've spoken to mayors and civic councils in Asia, India and South America. I go out there, I go big and it brings more people on board. After all, it's what I do. Whether it's light shows or bikes I've always been able to scale it up and make it work.

Even if there's resistance initially, there's always an angle you can use. I was in Santiago in Chile for the World Bike Forum in 2016 and I rode with Claudio Orrego, the then-mayor, and was interviewed on TV. I said all my usual stuff about how the world could be a much better place and how bikes can get us there, but do you know what stood out? Do you know what one thing everyone talked about and remembered? I said: "Don't screw this up like we did in the US." That ended up on rotation on the news everywhere for days afterwards. Because of how they perceived America, people weren't expecting an American to say something like that, but they identified with what I was saying – it broke down the barriers. They were stopping me wherever I went after that.

When we started back in the 1980s there were only a few countries where we could sell mountain bikes. Wherever you go now though there are people with disposable incomes who want nice stuff, who want a better life and all over the world there is the issue of mobility and the realization that bikes improve people's lives. Which in turn means the world is becoming so much bigger in terms of where you can take ideas and dreams.

Let's kick up a stink to get things fixed though, because we have to get people thinking about bikes in a positive way. We need to create a movement, a dance and a groove that makes people feel good, gets their hearts pumping and breaks down barriers.

THE CARS, THE COPS, THE CONCRETE AND ALFRED SLOAN...

People's relationship with their cars is scary. John Finley Scott – the dude who made the 1953 woodsie bike – used to talk about it very rationally. He said the car was a very efficient projection of status and personality and he was totally right. You see people in their cars and it's like: "This is my face, this is my body, this is my financial status. Watch how I move, feel my power, look how rich I am compared to you." So much of that is just bullshit though. If you've got the credit rating you can create whatever illusion you want on the road, even if you go home to a shack and a stack of bills you can't pay. There are a whole bunch of issues to tackle if we're going to make our world a better place but the biggest one I see every day is how dominant the car has become. Not just in how we move, but how we behave and how we prioritize stuff in our lives.

You see these massive SUVs being used for school runs, because they 'feel safe'. Yet those monsters create so much more pollution than a small compact car and if they hit a kid who's riding a bike or walking it's game over. For some drivers, every red light is a start line; driving's become a substitute for real recreation. It's a sport, although you don't have to be fit and healthy to feel powerful on the road, you just need a heavy foot and a lot of horsepower. But that's an illusion too. Vehicles are sold on this image of speed and power but most of the time drivers are nose-to-tail in a jam and that's when people really lose their shit.

THE PROBLEM WAS THAT – MAYBE DELIBERATELY – THE AUTOMOBILE GUYS TURNED BIKES FROM TOOLS INTO TOYS.

222

The craziest thing is that cars aren't even a good way of transporting people efficiently. The standard occupancy is 1.3 people so we've just got huge traffic jams full of half-empty cars choking our cities. Literally choking them. It's a huge problem. Driving everywhere is terrible for our health and it's so obvious.

Not only is car-based transport inefficient and unhealthy for bodies and brains it makes zero sense financially. The car is the second biggest expenditure for most families after property. But property generally increases in value, while the financial worth of a car falls off a cliff as soon as you turn that key in the ignition. Provision for cars even makes property more expensive too. It drives up the cost of real estate because whatever you build – workplaces, schools, shopping centers, restaurants, housing, stadiums, even parks – parking is an 'essential'. We are wasting so much money and so much prime real estate on cars it's just crazy.

When you talk about reducing car use you've got to realize that we're fighting against an incredibly powerful and well-funded opposition. The car industry is such a key part of the current economic landscape that they're very powerful and well-supported politically too. There was a paper in *The Lancet* – one of the world's leading medical journals – about how the petrochemical, fossil fuel and auto industries get literally trillions of dollars of government funding and support. People have been fighting wars over oil for decades. Thousands and thousands of people have died to fill our cars with gas. That's the level of funding and influence we're dealing with and fighting against here.

The oil and auto guys have also been working on discrediting the evidence of climate change and the dangers of car dependency for decades, because they know how dangerous it is to them. The people involved certainly aren't dumb either. Alfred Sloan was the president and chairman of General Motors from 1937 through to the '60s, and he was a genius. Like any smart dealer he knew that dependency was the way to create longstanding customers. He introduced the idea of model years for cars and suddenly there was always a reason to buy a new car every 12 months. He set up a General Motors loan company so people could buy these vehicles and live the dream instantly while paying it off slowly. He pioneered the concept of having a range of different brands at different prices under the same overall control, making it easy to move from a Chevrolet to a Pontiac to an Oldsmobile or a Buick. Then if you really hit the jackpot you could get a Cadillac. Even if people didn't know where you worked or what your job title was, they could see how 'successful' you were just by looking at your car.

I mean come on, let's be honest here, that's really smart and that's exactly what we've done with the bike industry. At MountainBikes we deliberately created a high-end aspirational product and I'm proud of that. We wouldn't even have had klunkers to start working with without Sloan and his designers either because the balloon-tired cruiser bike became so popular in the USA because of balloon-tired automobiles.

CARS DON'T MAKE US FAST, THEY JUST MAKE US FURIOUS.

They killed the speed and distance bikes could go. Cruisers looked cool but were heavy and slow. They hid the bike's true potential, so as soon as kids could get a real car they did. By the '60s and '70s bicycles of any type were only just hanging on. They weren't in the psyche except as something for kids.

ALFRED SLOAN

Sloan did the same thing with other transport systems. He bought up a whole load of public transport systems all over the United States – trams, trolley buses, urban railways – and then cut them back so that they just didn't work anymore. That meant people had to use cars more – the cars he was selling. Even my dad was part of this 'plan' as an architect. Helping to build this brave new world of spacious suburban areas with drive-thrus, shopping malls and so on all linked up by interstate highways. Post-World War II the whole country was rebuilt around automobile use with no thought for walking or cycling. It seemed like a great idea at the time but, oh man, now we know it's a terrible idea for a whole number of reasons.

In California, the San Francisco Bicycle Coalition has been fighting against car-dominated planning for over 40 years. There are similar organisations like that all over the world. And during the Covid-19 pandemic we've had an amazing window into how things could be. All those empty, quiet streets. All that space. No cars, no noise, no pollution. We've seen how beautiful the streets could be and we've got to keep that momentum.

I've been aware of the issues since I was a kid. That's why bike activism is something I've always been into since the oil crisis of 1973-74. Then there were lines of cars around the block at gas stations and prices went up 400% and we were riding round yelling at people to buy bikes instead. I'm not saying that all car and motor companies are anti-bike or that I've always kept my nose totally clean when it comes to getting involved with them. Subaru sponsored the Gary Fisher team for a while but at the time they were involved in supporting a lot of mountain bike advocacy through the International Mountain Bike Association (IMBA).

They're not the only motor company to have got involved in the sport. Right now, Mercedes-Benz are the title sponsors of the UCI World Cup mountain bike series. To me, it shows we can work together if we need to and make the most of that opportunity to engage and change. I truly believe the bike can be a big part of the solution to our current transport problems and that's what I'm totally passionate and dedicated to now. I gotta beat that drum, make this noise, use the influence I've got and all my experience in making a difference to help change things up.

225

DON'T EVER FORGET HOW GOOD THAT FIRST TASTE OF RIDING A BIKE IS, THE WIDE-EYED THRILL AND HOW WILD THAT SENSE OF FREEDOM CAN FEEL.

BIKES REALLY ARE THE HAPPIEST INVENTION

"Riding a bike is the closest you'll ever get to feeling like you can fly, to feeling superhuman."

RICHARD CUNNINGHAM, CR-7 BIKE DESIGNER, THINKER AND JOURNALIST – SPEAKING ON THE *DOWNTIME* PODCAST

I'll never forget what my first bike ride felt like. I was only four when I got my Schwinn Spitfire bike for Christmas and I jumped straight on it and rode round the corner from my grandparents to my friend Arthur Robin's house. I was pedaling so hard to get there and I hit that corner so fast I barely made it. It was this glorious moment that hooked me into riding right there and then and it's just as vivid now.

Another moment that will always stay with me is riding my bike through a tunnel in San Francisco during the bike messenger world championships in 1996. I was in this massive, loud, crazy, fun group of riders and it just brought home how much has already changed about my world as a bike rider. I started out as this kid who was a dork and who used to race against just three other kids and now I'm part of the coolest gang out there. It still gives me the chills thinking about it. Cycling is this astounding, empowering scene to be part of, but you only know that if you've tried it.

WE'VE GOT TO PUT ON A SHOW AND SHARE THE MEMORIES OF THAT FEELING WITH AS MANY PEOPLE AS POSSIBLE.

But that whole arrogant 'boy's club' attitude shouldn't be a rite of passage. That bullshit where some old gnarly dude at the back of the bike shop ridicules kids, women or beginners – we can't be like that anymore. Bike shops are the window into our world and the thing we can't do in this day and age is invite customers into a greasy man cave. Let's have more women's cycling shops run by women and maybe more places offering great food in store for passing riders and visitors.

Making bikes for and selling to new riders is a totally different challenge too. Even among dedicated riders I'd say only around a third of them want to work on even the most basic parts of their bike like blowing up tires. You can see it whenever you're on a group ride and someone has a problem – nearly everyone will hang back and wait for the group 'mechanic' to sort it out. If you're dealing with bike novices those minor problems are a total deal breaker on the whole idea of cycling. But if you can give them a machine that always works and it lasts well and it doesn't damage the environment then it becomes a positive part of their life.

Europe has it dialed but we've had to go a long ways in the US to make better utility bikes. When I started at Trek, John Burke really liked the idea of spreading bikes around the world and I would go into meetings saying: "You guys make all these wonderful bikes that go fast. Can you make bikes that last and have real purpose?" But the first response from many of them was: "Why would we want to do that?" The sales guys didn't want them because historically they didn't sell because there's no culture of cycle commuting or utility use in the US. They thought that if you made a bike that lasted a long time then you're killing your own market because you're not going to be able to sell people a new bike a few years later.

They were used to selling a toy, not a tool. I had to teach these young guys who were obsessed with performance how to make things practical. About how to put together genuinely practical bikes like the Europeans do. Using light colored tires that won't mark the walls when you're carrying them up narrow stairs to an apartment. Designing chain cases that keep clothes clean. Using wider edged rims that don't cut into the tire you last pumped up two years ago when you bump up a curb. Riding positions that make you comfortable in normal clothes and give you good visibility and safety in traffic. Stuff that every utility bike has in Europe but that we had absolutely no history of in America because our cycle industry has always been about making toys. We used to take Trek folk over to Europe so they could go to these tiny little shops in Holland or Germany and get a handle on this whole new world from people who knew it inside out. It's taken a while for that to trickle through the designs and the dealers but the results have been great – and sales have been too because, again, we're opening up a whole new market who never thought about cycling before. That's the message we have to communicate: cycling should be sold to everyone.

That's why we've got to spread this show way beyond the hardcore. The perception that the only people using bikes on the road are Lycra-clad pain perverts is not a good advert. They see us slaving up hills looking like we're in agony and they're like: "Woah, that does not look like a lot of fun. I can think of so many better ways to spend my weekend." Mountain bike films and images that may look sick to us as riders can make mountain bikers look like irresponsible hooligans to other trail users. Or people watch Red Bull Rampage on TV and think "those guys are insane", when in reality they're some of the most calculating and precise athletes in the world. They have to be or they'd be smashed to pieces way before they ever qualified for Rampage.

I'm certainly not saying we should dumb stuff like that down, because that's the pinnacle. That's what draws people in, creates the buzz, develops the sport. But we should communicate that mountain biking and road biking can actually be very safe compared to other sports.

YOU CAN MITIGATE THAT RISK AND MATCH IT TO YOUR OWN COMFORT AND SKILL LEVELS VERY EASILY.

That's the image that we have to get out there more – that most cyclists aren't lunatics, running horses or hikers off the trail or car haters running red lights and riding on sidewalks. They're just normal, friendly, law abiding folks who are stoked to get out on their bikes and want to share how good that feels with anyone.

We gotta teach folks that you can still get significant health and mental gains and feel the thrill and freedom of riding even at beginner level. I know instructors who can teach almost anyone to ride a bike in under an hour, whether they're 18 months old or well over 80 years old.

LET'S TELL PEOPLE HOW MUCH OF A BUZZ JUST SWOOPING ROUND YOUR FIRST CORNER IS, OR HOW AWESOME GETTING YOUR FEET OFF THE FLOOR, CRANKING THOSE PEDALS AND FLYING ALONG FEELS – HOWEVER OLD YOU ARE OR WHATEVER SHAPE YOU'RE IN.

hildren and families are obviously the key to a bright future for cycling. I'm really optimistic about this. he work that Matt Fritzinger and others have done with school MTB programmes and races has been nazing. We now have high school mountain biking (NICA) and racing (with the NorCal League). The number young riders is almost doubling every year. It's still got a number of years to go to be something really g, but it's getting there. I think, in 10 years, mountain biking is going to be one of the major kid sports r sure. NICA and NorCal are already having an astounding effect. It started with a few local high school ams racing against each other and thanks to those races we've already got a mountain biking world ampion – Kate Courtney – who literally grew up at the foot of Mount Tamalpais where klunking started.

Kate started riding with her high school mountain bike team after first riding a tandem mountain bike with her dad on the trails around Mount Tam. Having such great support at school in a sport that was once a renegades-only deal was incredible. Her national championship wins and her 2018 World Championship victory has given a huge boost to media and public interest for mountain biking and the youth program, but it's about way more than creating world champions. What matters is the fact that kids want to ride now, they're excited, they want it. You're often engaging totally different kids to those who'd get involved in mainstream sports like baseball, soccer, basketball and athletics.

EVEN THOUGH IT'S WAY MORE POPULAR NOW THAN IT WAS WHEN I STARTED, CYCLING IS STILL MUCH MORE ABOUT THE INDIVIDUALS AND OUTSIDERS. THE THINKERS, THE ONES WHO ARE A LITTLE BIT INSIDE THEMSELVES, NOT THE TEAM PLAYER KIDS.

It's one of the few sports that has always had equal participation from girls and boys too and they can be on the same team. And cycling isn't confined to a field, track or a pool – it's the key to opening up places and spaces you just can't reach otherwise. Regardless of whether kids want to race or not, that's a whole other win because cycling works solo or in a group, fast or steady – it's such a versatile, world expanding activity to get kids into because it's not just about teams, winning and pure athletic prowess.

I was at a trailbuilders conference in Switzerland a few years ago and a guy from Denmark was talking about their kids program which mixes racing with skills challenges. That means more kids can shine and everyone has more fun. They make the whole experience super-positive too. They've got good music, good food. They want people to have a good time in every category. A decade back I remember being at a big marathon mountain bike race in the Czech Republic. The next day was for kids all the way from 18-month-olds going about 50 meters with their parents on these little four-wheelers right up to 14-year-old cross-country racers. They have races for all of them, and they have a scene going on with it.

I GO TO THESE YOUTH EVENTS ALL OVER THE WORLD AND IT'S ALL SMILES. MAN IT'S SO RAD SEEING PEOPLE INVESTING AT THAT LEVEL, IT FILLS ME WITH MORE CONFIDENCE ABOUT THE FUTURE THAN ANYTHING.

Of course the parents get involved too. They help out with organizing the events and the social side – just like my mom and dad did – and in that way they get more involved with their kids. They see their kids are healthier and more focused and doing better in school because they've got more energy, they're more alive. Maybe they even dig out that old bike themselves and start riding again and remember how it made them feel. I've seen so many old bikes on the streets recently, being used for family rides or for the first time on long solo rides. The bike shops are flat out repairing all these machines that haven't moved for years.

And while kids are the future, riding bikes is still awesome whatever age you are because it doesn't smash you up like running. Where I live in California we have this 'Dino Ride' where all the guys are in their 70s and 80s but we're still super-competitive dicks because we're all ex- pro and top class racers who were racing each other 60 years ago or more. I go out with those guys and I'm the kid all over again and it's inspirational seeing them smashing it and realizing how much life you still have left. In 2017 the *British Medical Journal* in the UK published a study that concluded 'cycle commuting and regular riding was associated with a lower risk (40-45%) of CVD (cardiovascular disease) cancer and all-cause mortality.'

TOO MANY PEOPLE GIVE UP WAY TOO EARLY AND 'ACT THEIR AGE' THESE DAYS. THOSE PEOPLE ARE THROWING THEIR LIVES AWAY AND IT'S A TRAGEDY.

If you speak to older people they don't want to see their kids and grandkids growing up in these dangerous, polluted environments. They have this vision of how they grew up playing outside and being more active, not being glued to phone or computer screens, and they want that for the kids today.

Again it's something we can start small and still make a big difference. NICA want a bike track, a place, a space in every neighborhood in the US – just like a baseball field. That sounds impossible, but you know that's not such a big ask if we approach it locally. For years at Trek we had a real issue with most of the staff not really understanding mountain biking. It affected our designs, our priorities, the whole way the business thought about riding off road. Do you know what changed that? We bought some woodland right across the way from the factory and we started building trails in there. People started riding trails at lunchtimes, after work, before work. They started to work building on more trails, they hung out at the trailhead before and after riding. They got involved and they had a lot of fun. Soon I'm in meetings and there's like seven or eight out of 10 people who are now real mountain bikers when before there were just two or three of us. That changed the whole way the company thought and that's what we need to do with the way the whole world thinks. That sounds a big ask, but it all started with getting that land, sticking a spade into the dirt and starting to dig.

Racing is an incredible way to connect too. I rode the 2002 TransAlp mountain bike stage race with Bryson Martin who worked for Marzocchi suspension and now runs DVO. Bryson and I still get along great, because doing that kind of event with someone really bonds you together. There's a television interview filmed during the event in which he says:

" I'M GONNA START CALLING GARY THE MAYOR, BECAUSE HE JUST TALKS TO EVERYONE. HE'S SUCH A GOOD AMBASSADOR."

Cycling needs its ambassadors now more than ever. Riders I've known and worked with like Paola Pezzo, Sven Nys, Jens Voigt, Emily Batty and Jolanda Neff are all awesome, they're legendary racers but their personalities go way beyond their performances. They really connect and make a difference, they turn people on to riding. We don't just throw bikes under a bunch of riders and wait for the wins, we run our whole team program to maximize that sort of connection and positive impact.

I'VE GOT FRIENDS ALL OVER THE WORLD, PEOPLE WITH GARY FISHER TATTOOS, PEOPLE COLLECTING BIKES AND MEMORABILIA, I'VE EVEN GOT A WOODEN SCULPTURE OF ME FROM POLAND CRAZY STUFF THAT I'M ALWAYS BLOWN AWAY BY. I'VE GOT SOME AMAZING FANS, I'M REALLY BLESSED THAT WAY AND I WANT TO USE THAT TO MAKE A DIFFERENCE.

But even in racing things are far from perfect. Just look at how women road racers are treated. Equal priz
money is still rare and they have to race shorter races on different days or so early no-one is around to
watch. Television and media coverage is often missing too. What kind of message does that send? The
potential for growing the sport is amazing but the way it is now with the blatant discrimination compare
to other sports – I mean, why would you even bother with cycling if you were a woman?

Mountain biking was a real change from the male-dominated sport of road cycling because we had wome
involved equally from the start. They've always raced crazy hard on the same super-technical courses
as the men and their races are nearly always closer than the men's races and often way more exciting t
watch. I've always worked with inspiring female riders like Wende Cragg, Jacquie Phelan and Sara Ballantyn
those three really paved the way. We had a complete women's road race team at one point and of cours
Paola Pezzo was massive for Fisher bikes and inspired a whole generation of young racers.

We must invest in kids, we must invest in facilities and we must invest in the racers themselves – men and
women – because that's how we create the buzz. If we don't value them ourselves, nobody else is going
to value them and value what we're trying to do. Winning over the people who have the power, the mone
and the influence is really key to making a difference, to build the facilities that'll grow the sport. And nothing
opens their eyes better than seeing their kids and grandkids benefiting from being on bikes. I've seen it tim
and time again in meetings I've had – it's the point at which you make the connection, when the resistanc
melts away. When they stop being a businessman or businesswoman just thinking about profit and potenti
problems and they become a parent or grandparent again. That's the game changing moment right ther

One lesson I've learned is that if you want to make yourself happy you need to find y
own dance, your own rhythm. To rebel a bit, push boundaries, find your own way and
the thrill of expanding your world.

WE'RE NOT GOING OUT AND MEETING UP IN PERSON **AS MUCH.**
**THE INFLUENCE OF TECHNOLOGY ON OUR
LIVES IS NOW UNDENIABLE.**
WE'RE SOCIALIZING MORE ONLINE,
**WHERE ALGORITHMS GROUP US WITH PEOPLE
WITH SHARED BELIEFS AND FEARS.**
WE STARE AT **COMMERCIALLY CURATED WORLDS** ON OUR PHONE
SCREENS AND WE WEAR HEADPHONES
TO SHUT OUT **OTHER PEOPLE**
AND SHOW THAT WE DON'T WANT TO **BE TALKED TO.**
WE LOCK OURSELVES INTO BOXES IN TRAFF
IN A TOTALLY ISOLATED ATMOSPHERE
WHERE THE ONLY WAY TO EXPRESS OURSELVES IS AGGRESSION
AND ANGER. THAT'S JUST NOT HEALTHY, MA
THAT'S NOT HOW WE'RE SUPPOSED TO BE.

But there are ways to change that, to break out of our boxes. Here's an example. You
a wedding or a dinner and you're on these little tables and you talk to the people nex
you to be polite but you rarely connect. You never go and talk to the people from other ta
You get on the dance floor though and everyone is going for it, you're all dancing to
same rhythm, you're having a great time. Some people are going crazy, others are just h
a little hip shake, but they're all letting go at least a little bit and it's a great feeling. You m
a real connection with people.

"I WISH
I WAS AS CONFIDENT AS
GARY FISHER"

PIERCE BROSNAN, ACTOR, 007

You don't even need to speak to anyone to make that connection. Most times you have no idea who they are or what they do. All that matters is that you're all having a great time together. That's exactly what happens when you ride a bike or go to an event. You've got this shared experience that makes you happy, makes you feel more alive, even when you sit back down you feel great and you go home feeling great. Dancing is also a brilliant way to connect with other people and I love having others get up on the floor and dance with me.

I KNOW A LOT OF FOLKS
ARE REALLY UNCOMFORTABLE
WITH LETTING GO LIKE THAT BUT I STILL CAN'T
THINK OF A BETTER WAY TO COMBINE THOSE SAME
POSITIVES OF DANCING —
EXERCISE, EXPERIENCE AND FREEDOM
— THAN RIDING A BIKE.
WE NEED TO SHAKE OUR HIPS,
STRUT OUR STUFF AND
MAKE CYCLING LOOK LIKE TOO MUCH FUN TO MISS OUT ON.
IT'S WHAT I DID WITH MOUNTAINBIKES,
WITH FISHER, WITH 29ERS AND STILL DO WITH TREK.
GET OUT THERE,
GET OUT IN FRONT OF PEOPLE,
DO THE DANCE,
MAKE A SHOW AND SELL THE SHIT OUT OF IT.

And the bikes themselves are way better than they used to be. The capability of even an average mountain bike now is way beyond anything we imagined back then and it's the same with road bikes too.

We've got carbon fiber, suspension, disc brakes, wireless electronic gear shifting, all this sexy technology that everyone can see is cool. There's a whole bunch of stuff that maybe isn't as cool but makes riding way more comfortable and safer like better saddles, helmets and tire designs. All we had back in the day were steel frames with Campagnolo components that hadn't really changed in three decades and leather saddles you had to ride forever before they stopped killing your ass. Now bikes look awesome and ride great straight away, even if you know nothing about them. Cycling clothing has never looked or worked as neat either. You can get to work stylishly and sweat free, ride a century and still walk properly after it, or just hang out in a bar after a ride and not feel like a freak.

Whatever you think of them, e-bikes are expanding those possibilities and bringing the entry level fitness barrier right down for every sort of riding too. I've been doing some work with Bosch recently and it's super-exciting to see a multi-national company committing to cycling in a big way. We're already seeing much lighter, more powerful and longer range bikes year after year in every category from utility town and cargo bikes to performance mountain and road bikes. E-bikes are simply opening up the enjoyment of riding to a whole new section of the population. My town bike is an e-bike now just because it makes things so easy and civilized. The shops love selling them because the ticket price is higher and because, more importantly, they're opening up a totally new market of consumers who'd never thought of buying a bike before. It's like mountain biking all over again, but with even more explosive growth and maybe even bigger potential.

IT'S KINDA IRONIC THAT THE LAND MANAGERS AND RANGERS WHO USED TO TRY AND STOP US RIDING ON MT TAM 40 YEARS BACK ARE NOW USING E-MOUNTAIN BIKES AS THE MOST EFFICIENT, ECO SENSITIVE WAY TO GET AROUND THE TRAILS WE USED TO EXPLORE. THEY'RE UNDERSTANDING WHY ALLOWING MORE ACCESS TO THE PUBLIC COULD BE A SOLUTION RATHER THAN A PROBLEM THAT'S ANOTHER EXAMPLE OF A REAL GAME CHANGER RIGHT THERE BECAUSE NOTHING SELLS SOMETHING BETTER THAN A TURNAROUND STORY.

It's way easier physically to start mountain biking than it was before. When we started, we were just heading off on dirt tracks and into the wilderness. There were no maps or marked trails and we were using bikes that probably wouldn't even make it back in one piece. Now you have outdoor and indoor bike parks, trail networks, trail guides and all this information online or in print about where to go and what grade of difficulty to expect. The bikes are accessible in a way other top performance vehicles aren't. You can't buy a race car and drive it round your streets and you sure as hell can't fire a space rocket out of your backyard. But you can go and watch a bike race and then go and get exactly the same bike as your favorite rider that same day. And when you ride that bike you can really feel a difference.

I LOVE SEEING THAT LOOK ON PEOPLE'S FACES AS IT HAPPENS BECAUSE THAT'S WHEN YOU KNOW YOU'VE MADE THAT CONNECTION, THAT POSITIVE DIFFERENCE.

That elated look in the eyes from the freedom, the exhilaration, the satisfaction that riding a bike can give you.

Spreading that message was the whole point of writing this book. It's taken a while to get together, but actually the timing has worked out pretty well. Covid-19 has caused many tragedies but it's given many of us a pause and a time to think. Now we've got all these people out there riding, taking a break, thinking. Hearing the birds. Taking a deep breath and realizing the air is sweet. Real sweet. It's such a contrast to all the usual "GO! GO! GO!" and all the air and noise pollution that goes with that. We've been allowed to connect with nature. It's helped us realize what really matters.

It's also opened up our eyes to how the world could work very differently. How easy it is for a lot of people to work from home and how efficient and more environmentally friendly that can be. In fact there's now a whole bunch of people who don't ever want to have to fight their way through traffic into an office ever again. It's shown us how we can communicate and come together without actually being together. How we can make a stand about issues that matter, even if we're standing on different sides of the world. That's what we've got to do right now, make the most of this incredible opportunity.

It's easier than ever to attend a planning meeting for your hometown thanks to Zoom, but you'll be amazed how few people are in those meetings. Even in a massive city like San Francisco, which is where I live, you can make a real difference by adding your voice. We've got lots of activists now and, by showing up, we have the potential to exert some powerful pressure for change.

Get involved to keep emergency bike lanes and sidewalks open. Make riding, walking and bikeshares the new normal instead of driving. Support the closing down of streets to cars and opening them up to cyclists and pedestrians. Make sure money being spent is used for the right things, not just more shitty stop and go cycle lanes. Cars should only be well behaved guests in your neighborhood and now we know how cool that would actually be.

NOW IS THE TIME TO PUMP THE FLOW, DO OUR SHOW AND GET THAT DANCE GOING EVERY WAY WE CAN.

Let everyone see that this a shared language and experience. Cycling is a party everyone is welcome to, not a crazy cult or a private club. Sure there's tribal elements, but for the most part people who ride bikes are great people. We look out for each other.

"Winning at Repack 1979. Racing was always the proving ground for the technology. I won a pair of Ukai gold anodized aluminum rims, cutting edge tech of the time. Good set up made all the difference in the early days. Nowadays bikes are so much better, there's simply no limits!"

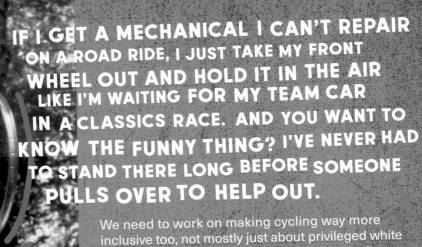

IF I GET A MECHANICAL I CAN'T REPAIR ON A ROAD RIDE, I JUST TAKE MY FRONT WHEEL OUT AND HOLD IT IN THE AIR LIKE I'M WAITING FOR MY TEAM CAR IN A CLASSICS RACE. AND YOU WANT TO KNOW THE FUNNY THING? I'VE NEVER HAD TO STAND THERE LONG BEFORE SOMEONE PULLS OVER TO HELP OUT.

We need to work on making cycling way more inclusive too, not mostly just about privileged white males who can afford a fancy toy. Organizations like Black Girls Do Bikes are a great example and model of creating bike communities for specific groups that may be new to cycling. There are now Black Girls Do Bikes chapters all over the US, all spearheaded by a local person who takes the lead to organize rides. I loved meeting them at the Trek 100 and hearing about how they share their joy for bikes with all women, especially women and girls of color.

Whoever we are, however we ride, we have to share our love of cycling and recruit other riders. Let's say hi to other cyclists, whatever bikes they're on. Put aside some time to lead a ride for beginners or take some kids out. If there's a local cycling for beginners scheme – get involved. If there isn't one, start one! If you ride with somebody new, put them on your bike, not an old heap of shit. Encourage them, give them the best experience you can, the wide-eyed, wonderful experience that got you hooked. Because everyone we get riding makes the party bigger and more fun and even if they end up dancing to a different tune, they're still up and dancing.

You got to take everything you can and amplify it really hard to get any kind of notice these days. And at the same time, you need to make whatever you're selling delicious. It has to look and taste so mind-blowingly good people can't get enough of it. Bikes are so much fun. They're really good for you physically and mentally, they save you money and they save the world too. As my story shows, that's a cool dance to know the moves to and an awesome party to hand out invites for.

IMAGE CREDITS AND CAPTIONS

Gary Fisher Library – GFL
Robert Fisher – RF
Dean Bradley – DB
Wende Cragg (Rolling Dinosaur Archive) – WC
Larry Cragg (Rolling Dinosaur Archive) – LC
Ray Baltar – RB
Steve Behr (Stockfile) – SB
David Epperson – DE
Arne Ryason – AR
Joe Murray – JM

5 • Marin County, 1981 – AR
7 • Where's Gary? Crested Butte, Colorado, 1980 – DE
9 • Young 'Red' at Lake Tahoe, 1959 – RF/GFL
10 • The Leavitt family way back when – GFL
11/13 • Great-Grandpa Leavitt's railway in Montana – GFL
15 • The Leavitt family, with young Saloma, Uncle Freddy and Uncle Johnny in the front – GFL
16 • Fred Applegate with Joan Crawford and Saloma – GFL
17 • Fred on set with Basil Rathbone on his 'horse', 1943 – GFL
19 • Various 1940s Hollywood film sets – GFL
21 • Gary, Resada to the Sea, 1980 – DB
22 • Saloma Fisher, 1950s Hollywood promo shots – GFL
23 • Saloma as a club singer in Guam, 1952 – GFL
23 • Military passport, 1951 – GFL
24 • Gary with Saloma in Guam US military base, 1953 – GFL
25 • Disneyland, the real one and the one in the yard, 1959 – GFL
26 • Slide shows with Fred and birthday parties – GFL
27 • *Family:* Robert Fisher etching, 1954 – RF/GFL
28 • Robert Fisher photographs, various early 1960s Californian bike races – RF/GFL
29 • Scene from a 'creative' childhood – RF/GFL
30 • Gary aged 17, 1968 – GFL
32 • Rick Fisher on his racer and with Gary and friends – GFL
33 • Saloma Fisher, a homemade speaker cab and pot – GFL
34 • Speedway Meadows, 1963 – RF/GFL
35 • Hellyer Park Velodrome, San Jose, 1963 – RF/GFL
36 • Hellyer Velodrome, San Jose, 1963 – RF/GFL
37 • Larry Walpole pushes off, 1962 – RF/GFL
38 • Gary, Speedway Meadows, 1963 – RF/GFL
39 • Marcello Mugelli, 1963 – RF/GFL
41 • Top: Gary fixing slot cars in his bedroom
41 • Bottom: 1960s club run with Mom and Dad – RF/GFL
42-45 • Various races in California, 1963/64 – RF/GFL
46 • Andy Johannasen, Steve Lubin and Gary by the car and in Gary's grandparents' living room, 1965 – GFL
48-50 • Senior high school year hanging-out with the Redwood Weed Society, 1968 – GFL
51 • Dark room tricks at Gary's home in Belvedere, 1966 – GFL
52 • Gary's first racing bike: the Legnano, 1963 – RF/GFL
52 • Euro influences started early – RF/GFL
53 • On the way to a race, 1964 – RF/GFL
55 • Munchkin hat, 1968 – GFL
56 • Tour Del Mar flyer, 1966 – GFL
57 • I.D.E.S (Sociedade Da Irmindade do Divino Espirito Santo), Hall 1966 – GFL
59/60 • Pranksters' light show, 1968 – GFL
61 • Pranksters' light show warehouse, Sausalito, 1968 – GFL
62 • Making slides in Gary's teenage bedroom and a stack of plates for the light show, 1968 – GFL
63 • Original light show slide – GFL
65 • Crosby, Stills, Nash & Young on stage at The Altamont Speedway Free Festival, with Bear's sound system, 1969 – GFL

66 • Ron 'Pigpen' McKernan, founder member of the Grateful Dead, outside 710 Ashbury Street, 1967 – GFL
67 • Bob Weir, Grateful Dead founder member, getting dressed up for the Freak Party at the Winterland, Halloween 1967 – GF
68 • Carousel Ballroom poster art and breakfast with friend Spike Goheen, 1968 – GFL
70 • Janis Joplin in Golden Gate Park with Big Brother and the Holding Company, 1967 – GFL
71 • Grateful Dead roadie at Altamont 1969 – GFL
73 • Bob Weir in Golden Gate Park, 1967 – GFL
75 • Mick Jagger in the crowd at Altamont, 1969 – GFL
76/77 • Crowd at Altamont, 1969 – GFL
78 • 'The Cube' lighting test tent, Forest Knowles, 1969 – GFL
80 • The Metro Truck, 1970 – GFL
82-84 • Fixing up the truck and riding out with Berry Allen – GFL
84 • Second place in the Tour of Nevada City, 1973 – GFL
85 • Tour of Nevada City, 1974 – GFL
86 • Racing cyclo-cross at Tilden Park in Berkeley, 1980 – WC
86 • Repack (l to r) Charlie Kelly, Chris McManus (beard), Alan Bonds, Joe Breeze, Gordon Burns, Art Black and Gary, 1977 – WC
89 • Riding in the Sierras with Jobst Brandt, Jim Westby, Tom Ritchey, Marc Brandt and others, 1974 – GFL
91 • *Bicycling* magazine, 1977 – GFL
93 • Racing, 1970s style – GFL
94 • Charlie 'I'd Rather Be Klunking' Kelly, 1979 – WC
95 • Frisbee Knoll, left to right: Benny Heinricks, Alan Bonds, Jim Stern, Alan's dog Ariel and Vince Carlton, 1977 – LC
96 • Scott Nicol adjusts the brakes on his Cooks Bros bike, Sea Tunnel Rock, 1981 – WC
97 • Gary in the pages of sports daily *L'Équipe* when in France as a mechanic and trading Levis for tubular tires, 1979 – GFL
98 • Exelu tandem drum brake hub off the original klunker – GFL
99 • Gary taking a break at Repack, late 1970s – WC
101 • Gary's original klunker – the front end, wheel and hand position are remarkably similar to current MTB geometry – SB
102 • KPIX's Steve Fox interviews Gary, 1979 – LC
104 • Mount Barnabe, 1977 – WC
105 • Repack, Serpentine Hill, 1977 – LC
107 • Repack. Various folks including Joe Breeze bottom left at Camera Corner, 1978 – WC
109 • Early MountainBikes press shots by Ray Baltar – RB/GFL
111 • Mount Tamalpais with Charlie Kelly, 1981 – DE
113 • Dennis 'Wiz' Leonard, San Anselmo, 1980 – AR
115 • Gary getting 'loose with the leg' looking for the fastest line on Mt. Tam, 1981 – DE
117 • Cyclo-cross race, Santa Cruz, 1980 – GFL
118/119 • Inside John Finley Scott's double decker bus, and the Resada to the Sea startline, 1980 – DB
121 • From top: Denise Caramagno, the Hipster Postman, Craig Mitchell and Victor Vicente of America, 1980 – DB
122 • Mount Gothic from a truck, 1978 and Gary, Joe Breeze and Monte Ward at San Rafael Reef, 1980 – WC

DATES
AND DETAILS

1950 – Gary is born in Oakland, California. At six months old, moves to the Pacific island of Guam due to father's posting with the Navy.

1953 – Mom Saloma Fisher becomes a night club singer in Guam and starts getting attention from one of the island's 'big boss men'. Gary's father gets really jealous and they split. Gary moves back to his grandfather's house in Beverly Hills with his mom.

1954 – Gets his first bike, a Schwinn Spitfire.

1955 – Moves to 47th Ave in the Sunset district of San Francisco.

1962 – Gets first serious racing bike, a Legnano with Campagnolo components. First road and track racing experiences.

1963 – A real big riding year – 85-100 mile rides with the club and competes in around 30 races.

1964 – First job, in San Mateo bike shop.

1966 – Becomes Cat. A junior racer with regular top five finishes. Gary's 'attitude and appearance' causes trouble. Eventually banned from racing for 'having long hair.' Meets the Grateful Dead for the first time in July.

1967 – While still at Redwood High School in Marin County comes across the Larkspur Canyon Gang and starts riding off-road. Leaves home at the same time and starts working on light shows for the Grateful Dead.

1968 – As the scene reaches its height, spends six glorious months running the Carousel Ballroom and living in Ashbury St. commune.

1970 – With the scene starting to disintegrate and the Grateful Dead now successful enough to have their own houses, moves out of the commune and heads back to Marin County.

1971 – Starts racing again and hooks up with the Larkspur Canyon Gang once more.

1972 – Meets Charlie Kelly. They each have the same bike and the same interests. They become roommates.

1973 – Finishes second in the Tour of Nevada City and becomes a Cat. 1 racer.

1974 – Builds his first derailleur-geared 'klunker'.

1976 – Starts working for *Bicycling* magazine as a bike tester. Wins the Tour of Klamath Lake, an Olympic development race, and places 12th in the national road race championships.

1977 – Places fifth at the cyclo-cross nationals, finishes the Red Zinger stage race and sets the fastest ever time at the Repack. Starts work at Sunshine bike works in Fairfax and meets Craig Mitchell and Joe Murray.

1978 – Rides at Crested Butte in the third annual Pearl Pass Tour, wins Repack again and the solo category of the Davis Double Century, in nine hours and 18 minutes.

1979 – Sets up MountainBikes with Charlie Kelly and makes first 160 bikes. Comes third in the Western division road racing rankings.

1980 – Introduces 'Bullmoose' handlebars, Shimano freehubs and 'Beartrap' pedals onto MountainBikes machines. Wins the first Reseda to the Sea race, The Central Coast Clunker Classic and the Whiskeytown Downhill and finishes second in the Northern California cyclo-cross championships on a mountain bike. Races the Coors Classic road stage race.

1981 – Wins Reseda race again. Sponsors a women's team in the Coors Classic. Visits Japan for the first time to set up bike manufacturing there, because it's become impossible to keep up with demand using US-built frames and assembly.

1982 – Wins the first Rockhopper Race. The MountainBikes team will keep the trophy for the next five years. Charlie Kelly leaves MountainBikes and company becomes Fisher MountainBikes. First Japanese-manufactured bike – Montare – arrives and proves a smash success.

1983 – Fits brakes under the chain stays on some models. Starts using steeper seat angles and shorter chain stays. Becomes a founder member of the National Off Road Bicycle Association (NORBA). A Fisher MountainBikes team including Joe Murray, Dale Stetina and John Lomis race at the inaugural NORBA National Championships. Lomis gets third. Gary Fisher and Tom Ritchey part company.

1984 – First mountain bike with Tange Prestige super light steel tubing. Adds a Shimano Dura-Ace freehub and toe clips and straps to the Excalibur race bike. Fisher team riders win 70% of all the off-road races in the us. Joe Murray wins the NORBA Nationals, Pacific States championships, Whiskeytown, Rockhopper and Ross stage races.

1985 – Helps develop SIS indexed mountain bike shifting with Shimano. Joe Murray adds a win in the Man V Horse V Bike race in the UK to repeat wins in the NORBA Nationals, Pacific States championships, Whiskeytown, Rockhopper and Ross stage races.

1986 – Adds the 'Bulge bar', super short 'hip stay' chain stay and wider 135mm rear hub to Fisher bikes.

1987 – Sara Ballantyne wins the NORBA World Championships and Mike Kloser takes the silver. Procaliber is voted one of the top 10 mountain bikes of all time in *Mountain Bike Action* magazine.

1988 – Fisher Bikes introduces first titanium mountain bike, the Prometheus. It is named best bike of the year by *Bicycle Guide* magazine. Also debuts the CR7 steel and alloy collaboration with Richard Cunningham. Mike Kloser and Sara Ballantyne take wins at the world championships in Switzerland and the Iditabike 200 race in Alaska.

1989 – Introduces Evolution 1.25in headset and fork with matching oversized tube set and seat post. Sara Ballantyne wins her third consecutive world championship for the Fisher Team.

1990 – Fisher Bikes debuts the full suspension RS-1 with Mert Lawwill-designed rear linkage, disc brakes front and rear and Campagnolo's new Euclid MTB component group. The 1990 Mt Tam becomes the first production mountain bike to use specific geometry for a RockShox suspension fork.

1991 – Gary sells the company to Anlen in Taiwan but things start to go wrong soon after. The first international Fisher team with world champions Walter Brändli, Albert Iten and Paola Pezzo. Montare bike introduces super short 15.5in (39cm) chain stays.

1992 – Alembic carbon fiber concept bike made in Japan causes a real scene at the bike shows. Gary secures sale of Fisher Bikes to Trek but remains closely involved with the brand.

1993 – First year of Trek backed Gary Fisher bike range, that includes 10 US-built bikes.

1994 – First Trek-built Gary Fisher range includes the super light Procaliber LTD OCLV (Optimum Compaction Low Void) carbon fiber race bike.

1995 – Limited edition 'Grateful Dead' version of Hoo Koo E Koo.

1996 – Paola Pezzo wins Gold at the first mountain bike Olympic race in Atlanta as Fisher becomes the fastest growing bike brand in the US. It introduces the Joshua full suspension bike.

1997 – Introduces Genesis Geometry to the team bikes, meaning a shorter rear end, shorter stems and a longer reach and it really works. Paola Pezzo wins the world championship and World Cup series while Gary wins the Masters national championship and a spot on the US Masters race team. Also starts as director of the Trips for Kids Marin, helping get children from cities out into the countryside on bikes.

1998 – Genesis Geometry standard on all Fisher production bikes. Gary races the first Transalp Challenge stage race, riding on a prototype steel Genesis frame and wins the over 40s category.

1999 – Paolo Pezzo starts racing and winning on her super light Golden Fly softail. Fisher introduces the X-Caliber disc brake 'hardcore hardtail' with 100mm Manitou X-Vert forks. Starts working on 29er prototypes with Mark Slate from WTB.

2000 – Paola Pezzo starts racing the Sugar full suspension race bike but switches back to the Golden Fly at the Sydney Olympic Games to win the cross country gold medal.

2001 – Introduces the Genesisters women's range.

2002 – Supercaliber and Mt Tam 29ers appear in the Fisher range for the first time.

2003 – Adds a Sugar to the 29er range but sales are still really slow on the bigger wheels.

2004 – Launches the Fisher Cake full suspension bikes as well as Dual Sport hybrids with 700c/29er wheels

2005 – With Freeride the hot ticket, Fisher launches the Kingfisher Freeride bike and GED hardcore hardtail. The Rig single speed also appears in the range and really ignites 29er sales – just when the brand had nearly given up on them.

2006 – Fisher starts pushing big volume tyres and long travel for trail riding with the Fat Possum. Cool bike, weird name.

2007 – Introduces second generation Genesis geometry (G2) with custom off set Fox forks.

2008 – Introduces Super Fly 29 carbon hardtail and Hi Fi Pro carbon fiber bikes.

2009 – Roscoe brings a unique twin chamber, push rod Fox DRCV shock and fatter wheels to the party. Both technologies soon picked up by Trek for their bikes too.

2010 – Rumblefish puts the Roscoe innovations onto a new 29er platform. Cronus and Ion road bikes also join the range.

2011 – Trek releases the Gary Fisher Collection, meaning the Gary Fisher brand as a separate entity is no more. Trek bikes remain massively influenced by the ideas and technologies introduced with Fisher bikes.

2019 – Gary writes a book about it all.

Authors' thanks

We've so many people to thank for the help with this book, but we especially want
to express our appreciation and gratitude to: Joe Murray, Mike Kloser, Joe Breeze,
Wende Cragg, Dean Bradley, David Epperson, Arne Ryason, Mountain Girl, Aaron Mock,
Joe Vadeboncoeur, Paola Pezzo, Antonio Colombo, Travis Ott, Rick and Debbie Fisher,
John Burke and to four people who are very sadly no longer with us: John Finley Scott,
Yoshizo Shimano, Dick Burke and A. Robert Fisher, Gary's father. Thanks to Guy and
Taz for the endless cat herding, the tooth-cracking patience and the enlightened vision
that turned a panicked e-mail plea for help into a publishing work of art.
And special thanks to our wives, Alex and Sarah, for all their patient support and input.

Gary Fisher and Guy Kesteven

Editors' thanks

Being Gary Fisher and the Bicycle Revolution has been quite a journey. And like all
long journeys it's been a fun, rewarding and very often an unexpected adventure.
We're indebted to Gary and Guy Kesteven for pulling this very personal and compelling
story together and to Claire Read for sifting through the eclectic and, one could say,
unique text.

The design team of Ultan Coyle and Alex Fergusson who took one colorful life and
made it into one hell of a trip. Muchas gracias Virginia Hernando who made light work
of a complicated production process for a cover that was brought to life so wonderfully
by Nico Rosenfeld, and to Keith George – as ever, our production hero – for making the
pages look how they were intended.

The visual history of the early years of mountain biking would be all but lost if it wasn't
for Wende and Larry Cragg of the Rolling Dinosaur Archive and the selfless work of
Joe Breeze and the Marin Museum of Bicycling. Besides shots of the fledgling mountain
bike years are some wonderful takes on Gary's off-road life from the likes of Steve Behr,
Dean Bradley, David Epperson, Joe Murray, Arne Ryason and Ray Baltar. Added to
the photography is the incredibly creative work of illustrative talents Andrew Thompson,
Matthew Burton, Ste Johnson and Japa. Gratitude to Linda Duong for making all the
pictures lovely. Lastly thanks to everyone at Trek, notably John Burke, Eric Bjorling,
Mark Joslyn and Sara Wilke.

Guy Andrews and Taz Darling